CHAMPIONS FOR GOD AT WORK

Champions for God at Work

David Kellett

Terra Nova Publications

First published by Terra Nova Publications Ltd, 2001

Published in Great Britain by
Terra Nova Publications Ltd
PO Box 2400, Bradford on Avon, Wiltshire BA15 2YN

ISBN 1-901949-15-X

Cover design: Gazelle Creative Productions

Printed in Great Britain by
Cox & Wyman, Reading

CONTENTS

Acknowledgements

This book is dedicated to my wife Julia. You have always been such a great help to me and I do not know where I would be without your support and advice. You have taught me an important lesson in life—that if a man wants to succeed, and be wise, he must listen to his wife! It is also dedicated to our children Davina, Petrina and Andrew—my best friends.

I am grateful to Dr. Kunle Onabolu for his helpful comments on an early draft of this work, and to Don Latham and Mike Ross-Watson for their kind words of encouragement along the way. I am also grateful to New Life Christian Centre in Croydon for the opportunity to use the material in this book in various seminars and talks.

1

THE CHALLENGE

It has been claimed that every time Tiger Woods wins a major golf tournament the value of stocks on the United States stock exchange rises the next day. Whether that is true or not, we all love to see a champion doing great things and performing beyond even their expectations. We all love to see a championship: it lifts and inspires us—and gets our heart rate going. I can still remember being captivated by the Olympic gold medal winning performances of the Russian gymnast Olga Korbut at Munich—even though it was way back in 1972. (I was very young at the time!) Never will I forget the sight of people, who were old enough to be my grandparents, jumping up and down in a sheer frenzy of excitement, as the basketball team at the university where I studied in the USA beat our rival team in the closing seconds of the game—to win the inter-State championship. Who could fail to be thrilled by a footballer like Michael Owen, that mighty Liverpool and England striker and goal scorer, charging through the defence (who are usually bigger than him) to score the winning goal—apart, of course, from the opposing team and their supporters!

Only those who have achieved great success as sporting champions know the feeling of winning a medal or championship title, and only they know the dedication, commitment, inspiration and perspiration that have gone into their winning performance, though we can all share in their success. Interestingly, though, Paul—that great communicator of the reality of faith—wrote about sporting championships to Christian brothers and sisters in Corinth, inviting them to see their lives like this:

> Run in such a way as to get the prize. Everyone who competes in the games goes into strict training. They do it to get a crown that will not last; but we do it to get a crown that will last forever.
>
> *1 Corinthians 9:24b–25*

To see their *lives* like this? Don't we mean their 'church life'? No! Paul was not talking about just one part of life, but the *whole* of it. For a Christian, this is about every aspect of life—home, family, and even **work**. The call to be a 'champion' for God is all-embracing, and it is packed with even more thrills and challenge than any Olympic game or football match!

Who do you consider to be a real 'champion' of the Christian faith? You may not think this a very 'spiritual' question, and prefer not to answer. But think of any great missionary who has made an enormous personal sacrifice to take the good news of Jesus Christ to people in some far off land: someone like Hudson Taylor, the Englishman who laboured in China, in the face of rejection; or David Livingstone, who spent sixteen years in Africa, and went back to his native Scotland with the scars to prove it (gained from a lion's attack, twenty seven bouts of jungle fever and many battles with slave traders.) You might think of Samuel Zwemer, who worked among the Muslims of Arabia. When his two young daughters died within two days of each other, he dug their tiny graves himself. Then he carried on with his mission work. Or you might think of Bruce Olson, who as a young man headed into the jungles of Venezuela to reach the Motilone Indians with the gospel. In his first encounter with the Indians they shot him with an arrow and punched holes in his skin with spears. He suffered amoebic dysentery but somehow escaped to find medical help. When he returned, they captured him again and he contracted hepatitis, but once again he escaped. After he returned a third time, he eventually found opportunities to share the gospel.

Then again, you might think of someone who has established

a great charitable work, such as George Müller, who founded orphanages in England, or Amy Carmichael, who established a work among the children of India—particularly the girls who had been forced into temple prostitution. These people made changes to the society around them—changes which impacted many lives for good—and their efforts will continue to bear fruits through the generations.

Someone who has chosen to stand out from the crowd because of their Christian faith may come to mind. Someone like Eric Liddell, who refused to run his preferred 100 metres race at the 1924 Olympics, because the race was scheduled for a Sunday. Instead, he ran the 400 metres race, and as anyone who has seen the film *Chariots of Fire* will know, he won. Or you may recall Wang Ming-Dao, who was imprisoned for over twenty years in China for being a follower of Christ. Despite all he suffered, he remained steadfast, and died as a follower of Christ. Lim Cheong also lived a life with zero tolerance for compromise. He was thrown out of his home as a twelve year old boy in Cambodia when he told his father, who made silver gods for a living, that he had become a Christian. However, he remained faithful to the call that God had made on his life, and God was faithful to him.

There are, of course, many of God's heroes and champions who have never appeared in books such as the one compiled by Harold Sala, *Heroes: People Who Made a Difference in Our World*. There are countless Christians who have not been accorded any recognition, but have still made a difference, because they followed God's way, despite the difficulties. They have taken the hard road. They have been determined to fulfil God's plan for their lives, and have matched that determination with action, choosing to walk one step after another in the direction that God has wanted them to take. They are people who have not settled for mediocrity, but have aspired to achieve something great in their lives by allowing God to work in them and through them.

What has all this got to do with working life? —a lot! To live out a working life to the full, and to do it God's way, is not an easy or second-rate calling. It requires us to be Christian 'champions'. It requires something of the missionary zeal of Taylor, Zwemer and Olson to reach one of the world's largest un-reached mission-fields. It requires something of the vision of Müller to want to change the world and to see God's kingdom established. To be a champion for God in the workplace also requires something of the courage, determination and perseverance of Liddell and Lim to do things God's way and to maintain God's standard, despite the pressures to compromise and the temptation to give up.

But many of us probably do not see the workplace as the place where Christian champions or heroes of the faith are found. This shows that there is an urgent and vital need for Christians to be equipped for working life with a clear vision of their workplace ministry calling, a clear understanding of its importance, and the power and ability to fulfil that calling.

Emil Brunner appealed for Christians to 'regain the lost sense of work as a divine calling.' Many contemporary Christian writers have also appealed for a new, or re-discovered, awareness of work as true Christian vocation. Larry Peabody has suggested that 'permeation' of the workplace with 'salt and light' by 'high calibre Christians' should have top priority, and that this calls for 'a new vision of ordinary work'.[1] Steve Walton reminds us that whilst professional clergy and ministers have been perceived as having 'callings', the work of anyone else has been termed a 'job'.[2] Sherman and Hendricks have pointed out that millions of workers see no connection at all between their activities in their workplaces and what they think God may want to do in the world.[3]

Work is an important part of our life. But its importance, as these commentators suggest, is far greater than its role in providing for our basic material needs, though that is certainly part of it. We have been made in the image and likeness of God, and He is a working God. When God created us, He established work for us to do, and delegated part of His work activity and responsibility to us. Our first 'great commission' was to manage the earth's resources on behalf of God, as He told Adam to:

---

[1] See L. Peabody, *Secular Work is Full-Time Service*, CLC
[2] See S. Walton, *A Call to Live: Vocation for Everyone*, Triangle/SPCK
[3] See D. Sherman & Hendricks, *Your Work Matters to God*, The Navigators, Singapore

Be fruitful and increase in number; fill the earth and subdue it. Rule over the fish of the sea and the birds of the air and over every living creature that moves on the ground.

Genesis 1:28

For us to work is therefore to fulfil a divine calling, ordained by God for His glory, and as a blessing to us. Tragically, though, for many of us, the long years of our working lives are lived out in a way which misses the mark that God has set for us to attain. If our vision reflects the physical and economic reality of work alone, but without the spiritual dimension grounded in biblical truth, it can seem like an endless treadmill. It can be filled with frustration, monotonous drudgery and toil. It can feel like a grind, which is just a means to an end—money, or prestige. It can be a degrading experience, a desperate on-going struggle, or even a fight for survival on the daily battleground of life; a joy-free zone, or something to be endured until retirement. If we are honest with ourselves, we are much more likely to feel thankful to God when our working week is over than to start the working week with eager anticipation about what God can and will do during it. Perhaps it is not surprising that only 2% of respondents to a survey undertaken by a UK bank said they would remain in their current job if they had a big win on the national lottery. One in five said they fantasise about leaving behind the daily trudge to work by winning that large sum of money.

In our minds, work can be the spiritual 'down time' in between our Christian services and meetings. We can see our work as the least spiritually significant part of our lives, or as the bit that helps finance the real 'spiritual business' of church based visions, ministries and activities. To be a worker in the secular world can feel like a second rate calling; that we have somehow fallen short of the ideal because we are not in 'full time' church based ministry. This perspective can be reinforced in our minds when we find that there is little or no attention given to workplace ministry by our church leaders. As Charles Swindoll has observed, very little is said from pulpits or by Christian authors concerning our working lives, which take so much of our time, energy and attention.

CHAMPIONS FOR GOD AT WORK

The responsibilities and opportunities we have as Christians in the everyday workplace environment are profoundly important to God, and the challenges and difficulties we face, if we choose to fulfil our calling, can be formidable. Our challenge is to work in a way that manifests the character of Christ, reflects the way God works, and brings glory to Him in an environment where others work to a different standard. Our challenge is to be ambassadors for Christ in an ungodly world by working to a standard of excellence, even though it may not be appreciated; to build positive working relationships with others who may be far from godly, and to live out an uncompromising Christian walk, despite the pressure to compromise. Our challenge is to be instruments of change, channels of God's love, and witnesses to the good news of Jesus Christ to others around us—and to be good stewards of the resources that have been entrusted to us as part of God's creation. Working people are, to use the words of Doug Sherman and William Hendricks 'the front-line troops in the cause of Christ'.[1]

These challenges require 'champions', and 'champions for God' in the workplace will walk closely with Him and show the courage and determination to do things His way. They will persevere to see God's kingdom come and, by His grace, will overcome the difficulties and struggles that working life throws their way. They will fulfil His purpose and plan by maintaining God-given vision, and by exercising faith along the way. Their work will be a worship offering to the Lord, pleasing to Him, and good—even if their labour does not get them a place in a book about great Christian heroes! But they will be people through whom the Lord will write history as He works through them to touch and impact the lives of people in the offices, factories, hospitals and workplaces around the world. When we look at our workplaces, and think about the people who work there, we can be reminded of what was said about Nazareth, the place where Jesus was brought up: 'Nazareth! Can anything good come from there?' (John 1:46). But something good did come from there. 'Champions' will be used by God to bring goodness, salt, light and life where there seems to be only harshness, strife,

---

[1] In *Your Work Matters to God*, The Navigators, Singapore

conflict, drudgery and greyness. In what seem to be the small things of day to day life, and from humble beginnings, they will be used by God to transform the ordinary into the extraordinary. Their workplace will be their mission field. They will be a spark of light in the places where it is desperately needed, and that spark will refuse to go out. Something good will result from them living out their working lives for the glory of God. Though they may never see the full impact of their faithful service, and may never be acclaimed in this life, they will leave an eternal legacy as Jesus is lifted up and the kingdom of God is extended. They will gain an eternal reward for fulfilling God's will for their lives.

That may all seem a million miles away from your daily experience of work! So, therefore, we need a vision of work inspired by the Word of God, a fresh sense of purpose in our work which is galvanised and directed by the Holy Spirit, and a new found freedom to manifest Christ in our workplace, to the glory of the Father.

This book aims to help challenge and encourage you to be the workplace 'champion' that God wants you to be. It is designed to be a resource to aid personal development and change by providing a structured and biblically based review of several key themes, along with questions to encourage personal reflection or group discussion. Chapters can be used for individual or group-based study. The book presents broad principles, so you will need to reflect upon how these principles apply to you in your own personal circumstances.

Working through these pages will not be enough! We need to invite the Lord in to transform this area of our lives. It is only by His grace that we can ever become champions for Him in the workplace. In fact, the closer and further we progress in our walk with God, the more we realise that *He* is the champion, not us. It is Him working in us, and through us, that will make all the difference in the world.

It would be good to see more books about Christian champions and heroes that do not just include missionaries and great preachers or social reformers (champions though they are) but also the testimonies of people from the ordinary offices and places of work around the world; places where God has done extraordinary things in and through ordinary people like you and me, living out our lives to the full for the Lord—wherever He has placed us. I hope, too, that we will see churches actively preparing and building up Christians to fulfil their workplace ministry calling more effectively.

2

THE BEST PLACE TO START

I remember starting work, after many years of study. It was a difficult transition, partly because I did not really know what to expect, though I quickly realised that I was unprepared for the very different pressures, office politics and protocol, and the very different way of life from the relatively free and easy university environment. It was also hard because the church that I was a part of at that time had no focus upon preparing people for working life. The focus was upon missions, church planting and the like. Nor was I aware of any materials or books to help. It did not seem to be one of those topics you raised with the church leaders, either. Nobody ever said you couldn't raise it, but it seemed to me at that time, as a relatively young Christian, that Christianity was about church based activities and missions work, and the working week was something very separate, something you just got on with on your own. Starting work felt like a difficult learning process, and after many years in the workplace it still feels like a learning process. As I have given church based seminars on working life, I am convinced that many other people, perhaps most of us, find working life difficult, and not just when we first start. Many of us find it a significant challenge to be a Christian in our workplace. So where can we look for help?

There are now excellent books available on the subject of

working life, and some are referenced at the back of this book. Various organisations and individuals provide seminars to help Christians to live out their faith in the workplace. This is all very helpful, and we certainly need more people in Christian fellowships to help younger or less experienced Christians deal with the things of life outside of church walls. The best place to start looking for help is at the revealed truth about God Himself, because He made us in His own image and likeness, and He is actively at work. The Hebrew and Christian concept of God is dynamic. Our starting point, therefore, is to look at how *God* works, and to see what we can discover from how He works. He gives us the pattern to follow, and there is much we can learn as we look closely at what the Bible says about His activity. Larry Peabody has pointed out that we need to have a clear vision of God's pattern—His way of working—and to shape our own way of working in accordance with this.[1] The biblical picture of the activity of God—His work—can be for us the source from which we can derive exemplary values, attitudes, character and principles which represent the best possible practice in work. God's way of doing things provides the model that so many of us are looking for, and which so many of us need. I wish I had understood more of the way God works when *I* first started working. It would have been a great help.

Once we are clear about the heavenly pattern for work, our challenge is to follow that pattern in a world that operates according to very different principles and values. But not only does He give us the pattern to follow, He also gives us the grace and power to follow it in our daily life.

THE GOD WHO WORKS

The Bible presents to us a clear picture of the Father, Son and Holy Spirit as the three persons of the Trinity 'at work'. The very first verse of the Bible introduces us to God as active, or the One who 'works'; the Elohim—the one true God, creating something wonderful in the form of the earth and the heavens and everything in them, for:

---

[1] See L. Peabody, *Secular Work is Full Time Service*, CLC, Fort Worth, 1974

In the beginning God created the heavens and the earth.

Genesis 1:1

The earthly ministry of Jesus also involved a busy work schedule. After miraculously healing the invalid at the pool of Bethesda, Jesus was questioned by the Jews because he had healed a man on the Sabbath day. Jesus made clear to them that he had work to do, and their legalism was not going to hinder his works of compassion:

> Jesus said to them, "My Father is always at his work to this very day, and I, too, am working."
>
> *John 5:17*

The Spirit also works. Part of his work is to help us to pray; to pray through us, and to intercede for Christians:

> In the same way, the Spirit helps us in our weakness. We do not know what we ought to pray for, but the Spirit himself intercedes for us with groans that words cannot express. And he who searches our hearts knows the mind of the Spirit, because the Spirit intercedes for the saints in accordance with God's will.
>
> *Romans 8:26–27*

Now that is a big job! Throughout the Bible, God has revealed Himself as actively involved in various practical activities that some of us may do as our daily jobs. In Genesis, we see Him as the 'gardener' and 'farmer' who planted and cultivated the garden of Eden, where He made a variety of trees grow, which were good to look at and provided food. We also see Him depicted as a 'clothier', who made garments of skin for Adam and his wife to wear. In Exodus, we find that God is the designer of the tabernacle, its furniture and fittings. After Jesus rose from the dead, He appeared to the disciples, and on one occasion he catered for them by making them a breakfast of fish and bread. Jesus was an excellent teacher, who taught with authority. He was also a servant who washed his disciples' feet, a doctor who healed the sick—though with the power of God rather than medicines; and he was involved in Joseph's carpentry business up to the age of thirty, when his public ministry began. God has 'worked' in may other ways —as 'military strategist', counsellor, leader and ruler, to suggest just a few examples. The Bible paints a clear picture of dynamic action—working activity—as flowing from Him. Let us, therefore, try to learn from Him how work should be done.

THE WAY GOD WORKS

We need a clear understanding of *how* the Scriptures characterise God's work. We need to look at the ways in which God's work can be, for us, the source of ideals —in terms of methods, values, attitudes, principles and character. His way of working is the best way, and the way that ultimately gets the best results; our observance of His ways will be pleasing to Him. Looking to the biblical picture of the way God works, we can identify the components of effective work processes. First, we find that His works are designed to fulfil a purpose or objective. Next comes the planning and organising, as well as the creativity and wisdom—knowing the best way of doing things. God's works are invariably of supreme excellence; He always completes what He starts; but He takes rest periods, which He schedules in along the way. He looks at the quality of His work, declaring it good; and the final result of His activity brings glory to His name. The creative act of God is so good because of His perfection; because of the goodness and love that are His very nature.

His works have purpose

The Lord's works are directed towards fulfilling His clear purpose and strategic plans. In Isaiah, we read that God sought to deliver the people of Israel from their oppressors, the Babylonians, by raising up Cyrus the king of Persia to conquer Babylon. God chose Cyrus to be part of this work, stirred him up and drew him into His plan to fulfil His purpose. The Lord said:

> I say: My purpose will stand, and I will do all that I please. From
> the east I summon a bird of prey; from a far-off land, a man to fulfil

my purpose. What I have said, that will I bring about; what I have planned, that will I do.

Isaiah 46:10–11

When Cyrus conquered Babylon in 539 BC, God allowed the Jews to return to Jerusalem. The Lord therefore worked in the practical affairs of men over time to deliver His people from bondage, to demonstrate His love and faithfulness to them, and to draw them to Him as their God. His plan was to prosper them, to give them hope and a future with Him, and through His work He sought to fulfil that plan. It is interesting to note that many people like to understand how their work fits into the overall plan or the 'bigger picture'. Working people can find it frustrating if they just do a small part of a bigger process and if they cannot see what that bigger process or purpose is. Many people need to see that there is some purpose behind what they do, and they feel motivated when they can understand how their role contributes to achieving the overall goal.

He is well organised

In the Genesis account of creation, we see how God created the heavens and earth as well as life on earth. He undertook a specific sub-task for each of the first six days. On the first day, He created light and established night and day. On day two, He created the sky, while on day three He created the dry ground and the sea. He broke the overall task down into sub-tasks or manageable chunks to complete during a day. Do you organise your work into manageable chunks that can realistically be achieved in each day? It is a good practice to adopt, if appropriate to the kind of work you do. There was also a logical progression in God's work of creation. He created the environment or wider context, such as the land, sea and sky early in the week, before making the more detailed aspects such as specific life forms in the latter part of the week. There would have been little sense in making the life forms before the environment to sustain them. He sorted out the fundamentals or overall framework first, then concentrated on completing the detail. I know from my own work that, before a particular improvement initiative can be successful, it is important to establish the context or infrastructure to sustain it. It is important to get people to see the need for the initiative, and to make sense of it in terms of how it affects them, how it links to everything else that is going on, and how it fits into an overall strategy. It is also important to get the basic supporting processes in place before launching a more sophisticated initiative.

He works collaboratively, with and through others

When God created man, He delegated part of His work to us. His plan was to see man rule over the earth:

> Then God said, "Let us make man in our image, in our likeness, and let them rule over the fish of the sea and the birds of the air, over the livestock, over all the earth, and over all the creatures that move along the ground."
>
> *Genesis 1:26*

He gave man something meaningful and fulfilling to do: to be stewards of God's creation. This calling gives us considerable authority, but also requires us to take on an enormous responsibility. In the New Testament we find that Jesus also delegated work and authority to others, and that he chose to work as part of a team. After Jesus had spent some time performing miracles of healing and deliverance from demons, he empowered his disciples with the authority to do the same, and sent them out on his behalf:

> He called his twelve disciples to him and gave them authority to drive out evil spirits and to heal every disease and sickness.
>
> *Matthew 10:1*

The disciples made mistakes, from which he helped them learn. Despite their mistakes, and the problems they caused him, he remained committed to teamwork and delegation. The most effective managers learn to delegate, and to support and coach those to whom they delegate. People achieve more by delegating than by doing it all themselves, and help develop those around them to do more too. The least effective managers are those who try to do everything themselves ("I'd rather do it myself, at least I know it will get done… I haven't got time to show anyone else how to do it"); and who find it difficult to work as team players. They tend to get bogged down in the detail and do not have time to deal with the bigger or more important issues, never developing the people around them to do delegated work. In general, those who find it difficult to work collaboratively with and through others do not tend to progress as far in their career as those who can. We recall that Jesus' delegation of work to others was an important way in which God's kingdom was extended on earth. He authorised and empowered others to work on his behalf.

He is creative

The creative nature of God's work is awe-inspiring. The psalmist reflected on how God forms each of us from nothing, praising Him —who makes wonderful things by His creative power:

> For you created my inmost being; you knit me together in my mother's womb. I praise you because I am fearfully and wonderfully made; your works are wonderful, I know that full well.
> *Psalm 139:13–14*

What space do we give for creativity in our own work? Do we encourage those who work for us or with us to be creative? The business world is looking for people to bring a creative approach to work, and to help identify the improvements that will help the company to be successful. Below are some quotations taken from job advertisements, illustrating the creative qualities that many employers are looking for:

> 'On a personal level you're an inspirational thinker, able to see the bigger picture and deliver tangible solutions to complex issues';

> 'confident, innovative and commercially driven'; and,

> 'your vision, creativity and fresh ideas will be essential'.

Not all job advertisements mention creative thinking explicitly, but many workplaces would benefit from it.

His works display the highest standard of excellence
When God made the heavens and the earth, His creation was perfect. Death and decay were only introduced after the fall of man, but God's original creation was good. So, as He reviewed His creative work at the end of the sixth day, He saw that His creation was very good:

> God saw all that he had made, and it was very good. And there was evening, and there was morning—the sixth day.
>
> *Genesis 1:31*

After walking closely with the Lord, Moses was a man who came to appreciate the awesome standard of God's work. Before the whole assembly of Israel, Moses sang of the perfect works of the Lord, to teach and prepare the people before entering the promised land:

> He is the Rock, his works are perfect and all his ways are just.
>
> *Deuteronomy 32:4*

Similarly, when the psalmist pondered the great providential works of the Lord, his response was delight, awe and praise:

> Great are the works of the LORD; they are pondered by all who delight in them. Glorious and majestic are his deeds, and his righteousness endures forever.
>
> *Psalm 111: 2–3*

Much of modern management is about creating processes, systems and working cultures to get people to deliver quality work to a standard of excellence. We have: key performance indicators; total quality management; performance related pay; competency based recruitment, training and performance management; Investors in People; Business Excellence, and many more frameworks and initiatives. Christians, however, should not need an initiative or process to be inspired to do excellent work (though of course such initiatives can help). When we see the standard of work that God delivered, our desire should be to do likewise in a way that honours Him.

He works hard

God works hard, to take care of us, and to work out His plan in each of our lives. So in Psalm 121, we read:

> He will not let your foot slip—he who watches over you will not slumber; indeed, he who watches over Israel will neither slumber nor sleep.
>
> *Psalm 121:3–4*

The earthly ministry of Jesus was hard work. However, his work for our benefit did not end at Calvary. His ongoing care for us is highlighted by the writer of Hebrews, who noted that Christ always lives to intercede for us. Our God works hard for us. In the same way, our desire should be to work hard—not to become workaholics, or perfectionists, striving for some unattainable standard, but to do a good job to the best of our ability—and in a conscientious way, with God's help. You probably find that some of the non-Christians in your workplace are well motivated to do good work, but not everyone will be—and that group may include some Christians.

He delivers on what He says He will do, and completes what He starts

The Lord promised David that his son, Solomon, would build a temple and be made king. When these events had finally taken place, Solomon acknowledged that the Lord had kept His promise:

> The LORD has kept the promise he made: I have succeeded David my father and now I sit on the throne of Israel, just as the LORD promised, and I have built the temple for the Name of the LORD, the God of Israel.
>
> *1 Kings 8:20*

When Jesus promised that, following his ascent to heaven, the Father would send the Holy Spirit, that promise was fulfilled— when the Spirit came upon the apostles on the day of

Pentecost. He is the God who completes the work that He starts:

> He who began a good work in you will carry it on to completion until the day of Christ Jesus.
>
> *Philippians 1:6*

He schedules in rest periods

While God works hard, and to the highest standard of excellence, He also schedules in rest periods. He rested on the seventh day, following the six days of creation:

> By the seventh day God had finished the work he had been doing; so on the seventh day he rested from all his work.
>
> *Genesis 2:2*

Jesus also saw rest as an important part of a busy schedule:

> The apostles gathered around Jesus and reported to him all they had done and taught. Then, because so many people were coming and going that they did not even have a chance to eat, he said to them, "Come with me by yourselves to a quiet place and get some rest."
>
> *Mark 6:30–31*

Many of us need to learn—or re-discover—how to rest. Many of us are caught on a treadmill of activity (work, church activities, family, friends…) and either do not know how to get off or how to say 'no' to more and more demands upon our time. Stress is commonplace, and when we ask someone how he or she is getting along, then we almost expect to hear 'busy' as the response. But God gave rest a priority in life. One day in seven is around 14% of our total time, but do you rest for 14% of your time?

His work reveals something of His nature and character

Psalm 111 is a celebration of the works of the Lord who provided the means of life and the means of redemption for His people. The psalmist pondered the Lord's work:

> The works of his hands are faithful and just; all his precepts are trustworthy.
>
> *Psalm 111:7*

The reason the works are faithful and just is that the God who did the works is faithful and just:

> They are steadfast for ever and ever, done in faithfulness and uprightness.
>
> *Psalm 111:8*

The quality of God's works is consistent with His nature and character, so, when the psalmist described God's works as great, glorious and majestic, powerful, faithful, just, and steadfast, he was celebrating the worker as well as the work. When we work with integrity, honesty, loyalty, patience, kindness, self-control or love, then we are working in a way that expresses the character and nature of God in a way that glorifies Him, and which points people to our Saviour.

He reviews the quality of His work

At the end of each phase of creation, God reviewed His work. After completing the creation of the sun, moon and stars, He 'saw that it was good'. (See Genesis 1:18). At the end of the sixth day, He reviewed the whole of His created work:

> God saw all that he had made, and it was very good.
>
> *Genesis 1:31*

After creating man, He reviewed man's condition and saw that he would benefit from a helper, rather than being alone. He saw a way to extend His work, and He created woman to be man's partner, thereby making His work of creation complete.

His work brings glory to His name

God's completed works shine forth as a testimony to His greatness, His nature and character. In Psalm 19, David expressed how the sun, moon and stars testify to the greatness of the God who made them:

> The heavens declare the glory of God; the skies proclaim the work of his hands. Day after day they pour forth speech; night after night they display knowledge. There is no speech or language where their voice is not heard. Their voice goes out into all the earth, their words to the ends of the world.
>
> *Psalm 19:1–4*

The psalmist also considered the works of God in helping, protecting and delivering people:

> Come and see what God has done, how awesome his works in man's behalf!

Psalm 66:5

The result was praise to God bursting forth from his heart:

> Shout with joy to God, all the earth! Sing the glory of his name; make his praise glorious!

When we work God's way, and to His standard; and when we offer it to Him as an act of worship, He is glorified in our life and we bring glory to Him.

This list gives a flavour of the richness and wonder of how He works, and it serves to highlight at least some of the distinctive features of His action. When we look at the biblical account of God as the 'worker', we have a model, or pattern, which we can follow. Our challenge is to grasp these principles, making them real in our hearts, and in the practical details and activities of our everyday working lives. Once we do this, we can be the role models for other Christians, and for our non-Christian colleagues. Not only that, but we will have a pretty good approach to work that will be effective and successful. I would have greatly valued such a model when I started my working life. It is one from which we can continue to learn throughout our lives.

SUMMARY OF KEY POINTS

1. The biblical picture of the work of our God—in the three persons of the Trinity—reveals the truth that He has worked in the past, works now, and will work in the future. God's work is not only concerned with the global and cosmic scale, but also with the practical affairs of this world and our lives.

2. God works in distinctive ways that reflect His nature and character as being holy, awesome, powerful and loving.

3. The pattern of how God works provides a model for how we, as Christians in the workplace, should work. Ultimately, we should work in a way which manifests God's nature and character, to bring glory to Him. This can only be done with Christ living in us and through us, and as we submit to him on a daily basis.

QUESTIONS FOR REFLECTION/DISCUSSION

Having considered some aspects of the activity of God, who 'works', you may find it useful to review the following questions, which can be used either for personal reflection or as a basis for group study or discussion.

1. Think of someone you regard as a good worker. What is it about the way he/she works that makes them good or successful?

2. Take a closer look at Psalm 111. What does this Psalm tell you about the works of God?

3. Think of some examples from the Bible of when God has been at work. What do His works tell you about Him? Describe some examples from your own experience that show how God is actively at work in your life, or the lives of people you know.

4. What do the following Scripture references tell you about the way God works?

Isaiah 46:10–11	Psalm 121:3–4	Psalm 139:13–14
Philippians 1:6	Genesis 2:2	Psalm 66:5
Psalm 111:7–8	Genesis 1:18	Genesis 1:31
Psalm 19:1–4		

5. What are some of the things you appreciate or value most about God as the active, dynamic, 'working' God; or about the *way* He works?

6. In what ways do people generally tend to fall short of the standard for work demonstrated by God Himself?

7. What are some of the effective or good aspects of the way that you work?

8. Which aspects of the way you work do you think you may need to improve upon, in order to be more consistent with the standard shown by God?

9. In a notebook, list the ways in which anything from this chapter (or from your review of the above questions) applies to you as a working person. Then list any **actions** you will take as a result of this study (e.g. further study or reflection, prayer, speaking to someone, making requests for help, changing something about yourself.) Be as specific as possible about **when** you will complete the action(s).

3

HANDS FOR WORK

Some people live to work. For such people, some aspect of work helps give their life more meaning. It could be the position, the power and influence, the money, or the feeling that they are part of an enterprise that is bigger than themselves. It could be the opportunity to develop or reach their potential that makes work meaningful. It could also be the opportunity to do their own thing that is exciting. The person who starts his or her own business, for example, can find great satisfaction in seeing it grow.

Some people work to live. Their work may not be very fulfilling, but they have to keep on going because they need to meet their financial obligations and responsibilities. For these people, working life is meaningful because it pays, and that allows life outside work to carry on.

Other people value the support network of friends that they can build at work, and this makes their experience meaningful and satisfying. Work can bring to our lives discipline, structure and valuable links with wider society.

But God has called us to an abundant and meaningful life. He has chosen us to be His sons and daughters, and to love and worship Him. He has chosen us to share in His eternal purpose, to bless us, to set us free, and to enjoy His presence for eternity. He gave us work to do as part of His perfect plan for

31

our lives. When God created man, He gave us work to do as a blessing. His desire was for us to rule and reign over creation as His stewards and to manage the earth's resources and exercise authority over the created world. This is the role that He still wants us to fulfil in our daily working life, whatever we happen to do as a job. When we grasp the truth of this, there is no longer any need for us to work to live or to live to work. We will work to please God and to fulfil the call to work that God has given us. An embroidered picture hanging in a friend's house has the following message: 'Hands for work. Hearts for God'. God made us in His image and likeness, and He is a working God. For us to work is therefore to fulfil a divine calling. Work was not devised after the fall of man as a punishment for sin, though after Adam's sin it certainly became harder! (See Genesis 3:17–19.)

By putting work into the context of God's plan, we will challenge the common assumption that work is a curse, a necessary 'evil' or somehow a 'second class calling'. Peter Curran has correctly pointed out that: 'work is a God-ordained part of our lives, part of creation's pattern and a key way in which we subdue the earth and work out God's purpose for ourselves and the world.'[1]

It is part of our life, and it is an important part. Similarly, by considering work in the context of our whole life as service unto the Lord, we will challenge a further common and mistaken assumption that there is a fundamental distinction between the sacred and the secular in our lives. Such a distinction can lead us to feel that work is the 'unspiritual' part, or the less spiritually important part. But by grasping the value and importance God places upon our working life, we can begin to grasp the reality of our workplace ministry calling.

GOD'S DESIGN FOR OUR LIVES

Before looking at the biblical basis for work, it is important to put work into a broader context. We have not just been created or called to work! We have been called to be sons of God, and our

---

[1] P. Curran, *All the Hours God Sends?* Published by IVP, UK, 2000

work is one part of life where the reality of our Christian identity can be expressed. It follows from this that when we see ourselves as called to be sons of God *first*, it no longer makes sense to think of secular work as separate from the rest of our life, nor to think of secular work as a second class calling. In this sense, we all have the same calling, all the time, wherever we are and whatever we specifically do as an occupation. Keith Tucci has emphasised that thinking of a Christian's work as 'secular' has put the church on the defensive, rather than adopting an 'offensive' or missionary attitude. So the challenge is to work out our Christian identity, and God's plan for our lives, in our individual situations, whether we are serving customers, building houses, programming computers, collecting rubbish, or being a homemaker.

We are a people set apart for God at all times

All aspects of our life are to reflect our fundamental Christian identity and calling to be, 'a chosen people, a royal priesthood, a holy nation, a people belonging to God....' (1 Peter 2:9). Through Christ, we are all called to fulfil this all of the time—whether in church, at work, when we are with the family, or when we are alone. None of us is excluded from the priestly role of living in the presence of God and giving Him worship at all times in everything we do, and honouring Him by who we are. We have been brought into continuous fellowship with God, as He lives in and through us. We are, therefore, a people no less 'set apart' for God when at work than when we are in a church service. Charles Swindoll, among many others, has challenged the tendency of Christians to divide life into 'secular' and the 'sacred' categories.

We are sons of God, whatever we are doing with our time.

In his earthly life, Jesus did not display any separation of roles and activities in terms of secular and sacred. Such a separation had existed under the Law, where only the priests could perform certain religious duties and acts of worship. Instead, Jesus lived a life of a servant in obedience to his Father through a whole range of circumstances. He was the Son of God, whether he was healing a leper, washing the feet of the disciples, praying, teaching in the synagogue, working miracles or making breakfast for his followers. There was no division in his life between 'sacred' and 'secular'. Similarly for us, as sons of God we are not somehow less than a son of God when we are at work—standing by the photocopier, stuffing envelopes or painting a wall. We do not have a more spiritual identity when leading worship at a Christian service. We have received the Spirit of sonship that transcends our daily activities and outward roles:

> For you did not receive a spirit that makes you a slave again to fear, but you received the Spirit of sonship.
>
> *Romans 8:15*

Every aspect of our life is part of our 'ministry'

It follows that if we are sons of God all the time, and if we are a people set apart for God at all times, then *all* aspects of our life, including the working part, add up to an integrated whole life of devotion to God, and a whole life service or *ministry* to Him. What good is it, for example, to be passionately involved in serving in our church but to be a manipulative tyrant to others at work, or to do work of such poor quality that it does not glorify God nor provide a good testimony to others? We are called to manifest the character and love of Christ and serve him in all aspects of our lives, including work, with *equal* zeal:

> Whatever you do, work at it with all your heart, as working for the Lord, not for men.
>
> *Colossians 3:23*

Note the word *whatever*.

BIBLICAL BASIS FOR WORK

Our attitudes towards work can be strongly influenced by how it looks or **feels** on a daily basis, or by the attitudes and comments of those around us. However, the Bible gives us a different perspective on the meaning and value of work:

We are made in God's image and likeness—as workers.
We were made in God's image and likeness to rule over
creation. The fact that we work is therefore rooted in our identity
as children of God. It is an essential part of being human, and a
vital part of our life of service to God. It is neither an afterthought
nor a punishment for sin. God commissioned us to work for Him,
before the fall of man:

> Then God said, "Let us make man in our image, in our likeness,
> and let them rule over the fish of the sea and the birds of the air,
> over the livestock, over all the earth, and over all the creatures that
> move along the ground." So God created man in his own image,
> in the image of God he created him; male and female he created
> them. God blessed them and said to them, "Be fruitful and
> increase in number; fill the earth and subdue it."
>
> *Genesis 1:26–28*

Against this background we can affirm with Larry Peabody
that all Christians should regard their work as sacred—and full
time for God.

For many of us, our work probably involves little or no contact
with birds, fish, livestock or the earth itself. It can be difficult to
see how you are ruling over God's creation and subduing the
earth if you are a hairdresser, computer operator, bus driver or
insurance salesperson. In the developed world, the economy has
shifted from dependence upon agriculture to economies based
on services and information. But whatever we do for a job, we
will be utilising the earth's resources in some way. We all use the
earth's resources, energy and materials, and we all have some
interplay with His creation—and this is inextricably linked with
our dealings with other people. Our call is to be good stewards
of whatever the Lord has entrusted to us to take care of. We can
thereby work efficiently, responsibly and in a way that is pleasing
to Him. As good stewards, we can also look for better ways to do
our work—to make better use of the resources we use, and to
ensure we do the best work that we can.

Work is not a curse
God gave Adam work to do, for his pleasure and fulfilment. He
gave him the Garden of Eden to look after, and this was intended
to be a pleasant task:

> The Lord God took the man and put him in the Garden of Eden to work it and take care of it.
>
> *Genesis 2:15*

The fall, through the sin of Adam and Eve, had the impact of making work harder:

> "Cursed is the ground because of you; through painful toil you will eat of it all the days of your life."
>
> *Genesis 3:17*

But the fall of man was not where work started. As a result of sin, we can certainly find that working life can be difficult, toilsome, and full of all kinds of trouble. We need to remind ourselves (regularly!) that work was intended, and is still intended, as a good thing for us to do—as a gift and blessing from God, and not a curse.

Your work matters to God

Diligent and honest work delights the Lord, whereas dishonest work and laziness displeases Him:

> The Lord abhors dishonest scales, but accurate weights are his delight.
>
> *Proverbs 11:1*

As we set our hearts to do the best we can, whatever work we find ourselves doing, we can expect an eternal reward from God as He accepts our work as a worship offering to Him:

> Whatever you do, work at it with all your heart, as working for the Lord, not for men, since you know that you will receive an inheritance from the Lord as a reward. It is the Lord Christ you are serving.
>
> *Colossians 3:23–24*

This is such an important principle to grasp. If we work to try to please people, we will sooner or later be disappointed. It is not always the most deserving person who gets the promotion or the biggest pay bonus. However, if our focus is upon serving the Lord through our work, we will be able to sustain good work even in the face of injustice. In his letter to the Colossians, Paul encouraged them to work at *whatever* they did with all their hearts. At work, we can feel like a very small cog in a very big machine. Our work can seem insignificant—but it is not. If you are cutting grass or hair, you can do it with all your heart. If you are repairing cars, do it with all your heart. It matters to God.

It is your responsibility to work—if you can

The Bible instructs us that, if we are able, we should work to provide for ourselves and for others. In Paul's letter to the Ephesians, he outlined the pattern for a godly life. Part of this pattern involved work:

> He who has been stealing must steal no longer, but must work, doing something useful with his own hands, that he may have something to share with those in need.
>
> *Ephesians 4:28*

Similarly, in 2 Thessalonians, Paul urged them to work:

> Such people we command and urge in the Lord Jesus Christ to settle down and earn the bread they eat.
>
> *2 Thessalonians 3:12*

It is also our responsibility to get our priorities in life right, and to live within the financial means that our work affords us:

> Finish your outdoor work and get your fields ready; after that, build your house.
>
> *Proverbs 24:27*

Having said that, there are some important forms of work that are unpaid—looking after the children, the home, caring for sick or dependent relatives, or even being a good student. Some people may be unable to work, or they may have lost their job and be looking for work, and other people may be retired after a full working life.

To work is a good thing

Working life brings many benefits, notwithstanding its struggles and difficulties. In it we can find satisfaction and fulfilment:

> Then I realized that it is good and proper for a man to eat and drink, and to find satisfaction in his toilsome labor under the sun during the few days of life God has given him—for this is his lot.
>
> *Ecclesiastes 5:18*

The encouraging verses which follow highlight the way in which diligent work can bring dignity, honour, authority, satisfaction, position, protection against poverty, and favour with others.

> Do you see a man skilled in his work? He will serve before kings; he will not serve before obscure men.
>
> *Proverbs 22:29*

> Lazy hands make a man poor, but diligent hands bring wealth.
>
> *Proverbs 10:4*

> The sluggard craves and gets nothing, but the desires of the diligent are fully satisfied.
>
> *Proverbs 13:4*

> Diligent hands will rule, but laziness ends in slave labor.
>
> *Proverbs 12:24*

> All hard work brings a profit, but mere talk leads only to poverty.
>
> *Proverbs 14:23*

While there will be clear benefits that follow from diligence, as Christians it is also important to note that the struggles and difficulties we face as part of our working life can also be used for good. If we walk closely with the Lord, and in obedient submission to Him, He can be at work in our character—moulding, shaping and maturing us, and cultivating in us the fruit of the Spirit. By responding to difficulties with patient endurance, we will also commend ourselves to God as we follow the example of how Christ responded to suffering. Peter tried to get Christians to grasp the truth of this principle when he encouraged submission to harsh masters as well as to the considerate ones. (See 1 Peter 2:13–21). To work is still a good thing, even when it is difficult.

Through our work we can have a positive impact on the world
The Lord has commissioned us as Christians to be salt and light in a world where there is little joy, love or hope. We are to be different from the world in terms of who we are, how we work, and what we say. If we speak positive words, rather than criticism and complaints; truth rather than gossip and lies; encouragement, rather than words that pull others down—then this, too, will make us distinctive. If we honour our boss, rather than join in the character assassination behind his or her back, we will soon stand out. If we pray for positive change in our workplace and in the lives of our work colleagues, and if we try to be witnesses for Christ, then we will probably be reaching a mission field that would otherwise be unreached. What an opportunity for a powerful and productive ministry!

Against this background, our attitudes towards work should not be determined by how it looks or feels on a daily basis, nor by the comments of those around us. Our view of working life needs to be grounded in the word of God.

SUMMARY OF KEY POINTS

1. To work is good, and is God-given. Through work we are fulfilling a God-given role to help manage His creation, and God has called us to do it to the best of our ability. That is an awesome responsibility and privilege.

2. Work is not a curse; it is a good thing. It was given to us by God for our pleasure and fulfilment, though it did become harder after the fall of Adam and Eve.

3. Our work matters to God, and through it we can serve and worship Him. Secular work is 'full time' service to God and people—if it is lived out according to God's principles. It is part of an integrated whole life of service and devotion to God.

QUESTIONS FOR REFLECTION/DISCUSSION

1. What total proportion of your waking life do you spend preparing for work, travelling to or from work, working, or recovering from work?

2. When we say someone is in 'full time ministry', what do we usually mean?

3. In what ways do you think God's original commission in Genesis 1:26–28 still applies to us today?

4. From the following verse, has work been given to us by God as a punishment, or as a good thing to do? —Genesis 2:15.

5. Read Genesis 3:17–19. From your reading of these verses, why can work be so difficult, and *appear* to be a bad thing?

6. Why do you think people may see work as an 'unspiritual' part of life, as a curse, or as a 'second class calling'? What advice or encouragement would you give to someone who feels like this about his or her working life?

7. Take a closer look at Colossians 3:23–24. How do the verses help you as a working person?

8. Under what circumstances do you think it is acceptable for people not to work to earn the bread they eat?

9. In what ways would you see your working life as a 'first class' calling, or as part of your 'ministry'?

10. List the ways in which anything from this chapter or from your review of the above questions applies to you as a working person in your own circumstances. Then list any **actions** you will take as a result of this study (e.g. further study or reflection, prayer, speaking to someone, requests for help, changing something about yourself) and be as specific as possible about **when** you will complete the action(s).

4

OFF THE TREADMILL

For many of us—if not all of us—our working life can sometimes feel like a treadmill. Some of the things that we do may not be exciting, and may even be boring and routine. We can feel a sense of drudgery as we face the same sorts of tasks and problems day after day. A mail order catalogue featuring toys arrived through my letterbox recently. One of the items depicted was a man dressed in a shirt and tie, crawling along the ground with a gun poised in firing position. This is the 'desk top soldier' and the advert headline reads: 'DECLARE WAR ON CORPORATE DRUDGERY'. The advert claims that 'the twelve inch plastic executive crawls along realistically, stopping regularly to fire his machine gun with sound effects and sparking barrel. Guaranteed to liven up any office.' A desktop soldier may get a laugh, and break the monotony for a moment, but it is hardly going to transform our working life from drudgery to joy! But is that possible, anyway?

YES, YOU CAN GET OFF THE TREADMILL

Nicholas Herman discovered how to escape the drudgery and get off the treadmill. He had a tough job working in a hot, smoky kitchen, day after day, month after month and year after year. He got little by way of material reward for his labours, and his clumsiness and physical disability made the cooking and kitchen work even harder. But he got on with it. To many of us, his job would look like an endless treadmill, and in many ways it was. The routine of buying and preparing the ingredients, cooking them, serving the food and then cleaning never brought him 'celebrity chef' status like many of today's chefs, because he worked in the kitchen of a monastery in the 1600s. Yet Brother Lawrence, as he is more commonly known, learned how to do his work, humdrum and difficult though it was, with great joy and fulfilment.

For him, getting off the treadmill did not mean retiring early, taking an easy job, slowing down a bit, coasting in to retirement or working fewer hours. The work itself, and its demands, did not change. But he escaped the drudgery by *practising the presence of God*. The key was his devotional life. He cultivated a lifestyle of worship *as* he worked. He practised living in the presence of God continually, whatever work he was doing with his hands. He learned how to abide or rest in God as he worked, gradually training himself to think about God and to worship Him regularly during the course of the day. As he learned a life of continuous devotion and communion with God, he found his experience of working life was transformed: 'I found myself suddenly changed, and my soul, which up until then was always in distress, experienced a deep inner peace, as if it was in its centre and in a place of rest.'[1] He got off the treadmill.

You might think that it must have been easier for him, living in some monastery hundreds of years ago, with none of the pressures of modern living. But there are some powerful lessons we can all learn from this man; lessons that will help transform our experience of work. So let us take a closer look at how he developed a lifestyle of worship and devotion at work.

Firstly, he learned how to live in the presence of God. During the course of the day, and even just for brief moments, he would turn his attention to God. He would think about God, speak to Him, pray to Him, worship Him: 'we should,' he said, 'fix

---

[1] E.M. Blaiklock (Ed.) *The Practice of the Presence of God*, p. 44 (1981)
Used by permission of Hodder & Stoughton

ourselves firmly in the presence of God by conversing all the time with Him.'[1] He learned, little by little, to turn his thoughts and his heart to God even in the midst of doing his most demanding tasks. Over time, he developed such a strong devotional life at work that he came to see no distinction between formal prayer times or worship times and the times when he was working at his job. He was in an attitude of worship and devotion all the time. Of course, he still had to do his job and there was no room for 'day dreaming' in his work. Practising the presence of God is not about having your head in the clouds when you should be working; it is about finding moments during the day to turn back to God and to converse with Him. If Brother Lawrence found that his work took all his attention for a while, he would simply turn his attention back to God when he became aware that he had broken his communication line with Him. 'Grow accustomed, then, little by little thus to worship Him, to ask for His grace, to offer Him your heart from time to time in the course of the day, amid your labours, at any time you can.'[2]

Secondly, he learned to do everything at work as an act of worship or devotion to God. He had to do some unpleasant and mundane things, but the task stopped being so burdensome when he learned to do it to the best of his ability to show God how much he loved Him. He found it a joy to live and work to please Him: 'But having taken as the end of all his actions, to do them all for the love of God, he was well satisfied therewith. He was happy, he said, to pick up a straw from the ground for the love of God.'[3] It was not easy. He had a natural aversion to working in the kitchen, but he sought to do all his work as an expression of his love for God. It needed perseverance and effort, but once he was able to live out his working life as a worship offering to God, there was joy and peace in his heart and a sense of purpose and fulfilment.

Thirdly, he learned to ask God for help. Sometimes, in the thick of our day, we forget that God wants to help us and give us the grace, wisdom and strength we need to do all that we need to do. God is interested in helping us. He is always there for us, but we tend to forget about Him once the working day starts.

---

[1] *Ibid.*, p. 19   [2] *Ibid.*, p. 42   [3] *Ibid.*, p. 21

When Brother Lawrence had difficult tasks to do, he turned to God for help; he acknowledged that God was the God of his work and everything he did. Once the task was done, he would then thank God for helping him through. Here is an example: 'He had been sent off a few days earlier to Burgundy for stocks of wine, a painful task for him as he had no aptitude for business, was lame in one leg, and could only get about the boat by rolling himself over the casks. He did not, however, trouble himself about this, no more than about his whole purchase of wine. He told God that it was His business, after which he found that everything worked out and worked out well. He had been sent to Auvergne the year before on a similar errand. He could not say how the business worked out. It was not he who managed it and it turned out very well.'[1] Much of the stress and pressure we feel comes from the sense that we have too much to do and too little time or resources. Brother Lawrence learned to give his burdens to the Lord and to seek His help. In the practical day to day realities of his work, he learned how to worship God as His provider and help by acknowledging his dependence on Him. How much do we depend on God in our day to day work? How much do we live a life of worship to Him as we work? Do we tend to leave God at home and rely on our own abilities and efforts to get us through the working day?

If we could only learn to worship and commune with Him as we work, we would be less likely to be found staggering through the day and just about making it to the end of the week. If we could learn to pray to Him, talk to Him, seek His help, worship and love Him throughout the day, we could get off the treadmill of life and be found filled with the joy of the Lord—even if we are peeling potatoes for a living! If Brother Lawrence could do it, then so can we!

A WHOLE LIFE OF WORSHIP

Every area of our life can be worship to God. Paul urged the Thessalonians to cultivate a lifestyle that was pleasing to God in all respects and at all times:

---

[1] *Ibid.*, p. 23

> Finally, brothers, we instructed you how to live in order to please
> God, as in fact you are living. Now we ask you and urge you in
> the Lord Jesus to do this more and more.
>
> *1 Thessalonians 4:1*

Living to please God is a desire that can begin to permeate your whole life. Bob Mumford has described such a change taking place, as he began to discover a deeper worship life. He tells us that when he first became conscious of the fact that he could afford God pleasure, a desire was born within him to be a 'God-pleaser in every area of his life.'[1] A whole life of worship is not just about doing more and doing things differently. It is about giving God back your life; it is about giving Him yourself in a way which says 'Lord, you are worthy to receive this and more'. As Paul wrote to the church in Rome:

> Therefore, I urge you, brothers, in view of God's mercy, to offer
> your bodies as living sacrifices, holy and pleasing to God—this is
> your spiritual act of worship.
>
> *Romans 12:1*

The question for us as working Christians is whether our whole life, including our life in the workplace, is lived as an act of worship to please and glorify God. Is our work done to the best of our ability and for His pleasure and glory? Or are we focused upon the work, our experience of how the work feels, or the rewards that we get from it?

WORK AND WORSHIP

Our work can be an act of worship, something that can be pleasing to God, if done in a way that honours Him. When we are willing and able to offer it daily to honour God, and as an act of service to Him—however mundane and routine our work may seem—it can be transformed into something meaningful, fulfilling and enjoyable. Our work can be changed into a labour of love toward

---

[1] See Bob Mumford, *Entering and Enjoying Worship*, Manna Christian Outreach

God rather than it being toilsome drudgery. The work itself may not change, but the experience of work can be transformed. When we grasp the truth of this, we will rise above the day to day circumstances, and learn to 'rejoice in the Lord always' (Philippians 4:4), even during our working day, and even on Monday morning! As Ben Patterson has said, 'as worshipers we see our work become a royal enterprise instead of slavish drudgery', and: 'work should be a form of worship—not of the work, but of the God we serve through the work'.[1] Work can therefore become something we do for God with all our hearts, lived to the full as a precious and good part of our life. It can be something to look forward to and to cherish as valuable, satisfying and meaningful.

Most people would probably question our sanity if we said we loved our work. However, when we learn to live our working life as worship that is pleasing to God, it can become meaningful—even enjoyable. We may even come to a point where we can say 'I love my job!' without expecting friendly psychiatrists in white coats to take us away. But if pleasing God is not our primary focus, then we are likely to find work toilsome and ultimately meaningless—a continuous and relentless treadmill. The writer of Ecclesiastes expressed this principle in very clear terms:

> A man can do nothing better than to eat and drink and find satisfaction in his work. This too, I see, is from the hand of God, for without him, who can eat or find enjoyment? To the man who pleases him, God gives wisdom, knowledge and happiness, but to the sinner he gives the task of gathering and storing up wealth to hand it over to the one who pleases God. This too is meaningless, a chasing after the wind.
>
> *Ecclesiastes 2:24–26*

As we serve God through our work and seek to please Him, there is also a very real sense in which we overcome the world. If we are clear that we live to serve and please God through our work, then we can rise above the circumstances and maintain a consistent walk—with our feet on firm ground. The circumstances of life should not trouble us any more when we

---

[1] B. Patterson, *Work and Worship: Serving God in Everything You Do*, IVP, 1994

know who our Divine 'employer' is, offering our service to Him.

We know our work can become an acceptable offering to God when we are prepared to say, 'Lord, I'll do this work you have given me to do for Your glory. I'll do it Your way to please and honour You. I'll give my best, because I want you to be pleased with this. I live this area of my life for You because I love You and because You are worthy of my obedience, service and praise. Let Jesus be manifest in all I do in my workplace. Bring glory to Your Name through my work, because I live for You. Let Your will be done today in all I do. Thank you, Lord, for this opportunity to serve You through my work. Be glorified now and at all times in my life.'

Getting off the treadmill of life is neither about escaping from work nor doing less of it. Finding the 'good life' is not about dropping out of the rat race of society and getting an idyllic patch of land to cultivate. It is about finding new meaning in what we do. It is about seeing life through spiritual eyes; and it is about offering all we do to God for His pleasure. Our work is from Him and for Him. Brother Lawrence discovered the keys to the good life, and we too can follow his simple example. We, too, can get off the treadmill and into something far better—God's presence.

SUMMARY OF KEY POINTS

1. Work forms a part of our practical day to day worship of God as we seek to do it in a way which is pleasing to Him, and which glorifies Him.

2. Once we grasp the fact that work can be an acceptable worship offering to God, we can find new meaning in our day to day activities, and a new passion to work to please Him.

3. The world is likely to be hostile, or at best indifferent, to our godly standards of work. In such circumstances, working in God's way to please Him can be a 'sacrifice of praise' —an acceptable and pleasing sacrifice to Him.

4. There is joy, satisfaction, liberty, fulfilment and an eternal reward for us when we live out our daily working life as a spiritual act of worship, as a sacrifice of praise and as a labour of love to praise and glorify God.

QUESTIONS FOR REFLECTION/DISCUSSION

1. Read Ecclesiastes 2:17–23. From your own experience, why can work seem like meaningless drudgery, a daily struggle or even a waste of time?

2. How would you define 'worship'? In what sense can your daily working life be offered as worship to God?

3. Considering the following verses, what will make all the difference in the world to your experience of work?

    Ecclesiastes 2:24–26
    Ecclesiastes 5:18–20

4. Take a closer look at 1 Thessalonians 4:1. As you consider this verse, list some of the practical and specific things you can do in your daily work to show you are living to please God.

5. Brother Lawrence described how he cultivated his devotional life while at work: 'Grow accustomed, then, little by little thus to worship Him, to ask for His grace, to offer Him your heart from time to time in the course of the day, amid your labours, at any time you can.' In practical terms, how would you go about doing this in your daily work? What difficulties do you think you may experience?

6. What do you think motivates most people to work well, or de-motivates people in a way that means they are likely to work badly?

7. How would you describe the heart attitude and behaviour of a worshipping worker?

8. What do you think may hinder your desire and daily efforts to live your working life to please God?

9. List ways in which anything from this chapter or from your review of the above questions applies to you as a working person in your own circumstances. Then list any **actions** you will take as a result of this study (e.g. further study or reflection, prayer, speaking to someone, requests for help, changing something about yourself) and be as specific as possible about **when** you will complete the action(s).

5

WHAT IS YOUR
'MISSION STATEMENT'?

'Excellence' is one of those words we see a lot these days. It appears in the mission statements of millions of organisations and businesses. From producers of garden products ('we pursue excellence in all areas of our business—in our manufacturing processes, in our products, in our services and in the environment in which we work') to a university ('the University is committed to excellence in learning and teaching'). From a manufacturer of health care products ('we are determined to achieve excellence and true world class standards in all our activities, through the continuous improvement of our products, services and processes') to a police department in urban America ('to provide excellence in public services through aggressive pursuit of violators of the law and the prevention of crime and disorderliness'). Excellence is clearly something organisations value. It is something they are keen to get the workforce to aspire to achieve. A well motivated, inspired group of workers focused upon a common goal of high achievement has got to be good news for any business.

In their now classic book *In Search of Excellence*, Tom Peters and Robert Waterman demonstrated that the most successful companies in America are better at encouraging people to give their best. Staff would encourage excellent work through their clear commitment to meeting customer needs, as well as through their approach to managing people. The authors found that these companies require and demand extraordinary performance from their employees and give them the autonomy and scope to make improvements, seeking to encourage 'armies of dedicated champions' to deliver good work and take the company forward by valuing their individual workers, giving them the scope to express their ideas and treating them decently. While 'people are our greatest asset' is now something of a corporate cliché, the most successful companies try to make this a reality. The individual is not lost in a whole series of processes, but valued as a key element of success. Treating people respectfully and giving them a clear understanding of what the company expects, and a vision of excellence to work toward, seem to be keys for drawing excellent work out of people.

It is easy to talk about a culture of excellence, but it is difficult to achieve and sustain. Certainly, lessons can be learned from how the most successful companies manage their business and their people. Good management will certainly help to raise the standard of work that people produce and bad management will demotivate, stifle innovation and even make people ill. However, no management programme or culture change strategy will inspire everyone to do excellent work. There will always be those who are disappointed by their managers and leaders. People will see inconsistencies and injustices in the way issues and workers are handled, which only serves to make them sceptical about how serious the leaders and managers really are concerning the mission statement and company values. If someone is not fairly rewarded relative to someone else for their hard work, are they likely to continue producing excellent work? If you take the carrots and sticks away, will people still reach for the skies in terms of their performance?

Ultimately, people need to be committed to excellence on the inside, in their hearts and minds. In a recent television interview, the British newsreader Trevor McDonald noted that, when he was growing up in the West Indies, his father always inspired him to be the best at what he did. If he were to be a milkman when he grew up, then he should be the best milkman he could be. Excellent performance will only be sustained if a worker is committed to being excellent whether they are rewarded or recognised for it or not. Good management can certainly help draw this out of people, but ultimately a heart for excellence is a heart that has been touched and changed by God and desires to follow His way.

GOD'S STANDARD

God's standard for work is our benchmark, and that benchmark is excellence. When He had completed His work of creating the heavens and the earth and all life forms, God looked at it and saw that 'it was very good' (Genesis 1: 31). The Psalms also testify to the great and marvellous works of God:

> Great are the works of the Lord;
> they are pondered by all who delight in them
> *Psalm 111:2*

One essential feature of God's work is that He always gives His best, even when His best may be far from appreciated. He gave us Jesus to fulfil His work of redemption, but Jesus was despised, rejected, oppressed and afflicted (Isaiah 53:1–9). This gives us the model or pattern for our work: to give our very best, for God's glory, regardless of how it is received.

If we look to the standard that other people around us may set or follow, then, sooner or later, we will be disappointed. It is good to respect those placed in positions of authority over us, but if we expect our leaders to always be fair, just, helpful, conscientious and concerned about our welfare, then we will be disappointed. However hard someone in a position of power and responsibility tries to live up to the mission statement and company values, nobody is perfect. But God's standard is always fair, just and consistently good: in short, it is excellent. Our workplace model should therefore be God's—not man's. We can learn valuable skills and lessons from more experienced and capable people, things that will help us to be better at what we do, but there is no model better than God Himself.

The key qualities of the most successful companies identified by Peters and Waterman tend to be that they are:

☐ Action oriented —keen to do, rather than just analyse, and keen to try new ways of doing things.

☐ Close to the customer—being prepared to listen to those people the company serves.

☐ Open to giving people the autonomy and scope to try new things, to innovate, and to learn from their mistakes.

☐ Good at treating people with respect. People are seen as a valuable asset who make an important contribution with potentially useful ideas.

☐ Clear about the values that drive the company, and excellent companies tend to be places where the leaders live out the values in their day to day dealings with people.

☐ Focused upon doing what they know best.

☐ Simply structured around some central theme, with the flexibility to adapt to change. There should be relatively few at the corporate centre.

☐ Organised around a few important core values, but push autonomy down to the individual and team.

When we reflect upon the way God works, we can see that the best practices in human organizations reflect His ways. He is action oriented. He plans, He creates, and He sustains His creation. He works in our day to day circumstances, in the lives of people, in practical ways—guiding, helping, healing, teaching, and comforting. He is the best listener we will ever know. He listens to our prayers, our worship, and our cries. Not only that; He responds faithfully to what He hears, because He loves us. He wants to meet our needs and to help us become the people He wants us to be. He gives us the autonomy to live out our Christian lives, and to make our own choices—and, sometimes, mistakes— giving us the grace to learn from the mistakes and to change. He values us enough to have given us Jesus, and He will never leave nor forsake us. His kingdom has clear values, reflecting His nature. He invites us to participate with Him in building His everlasting kingdom, which is simply structured—with God Himself at the head. God's ways are excellence in action.

GIVING YOUR BEST

The word of God encourages us to work hard and give our best to God, with whatever measure of ability we have been given. In the parable of the talents (Matthew 25:14–30), the master gave three servants some talents of money in proportion to their ability. While the master went on a journey, the one who had been given five talents and the one who had been given two talents put the resources that they had to good use, and there was a profit to show their master when he returned. They were rewarded for their efforts and faithful stewardship of the talents they had been trusted with. The one who had been given one talent failed to use the resources that had been entrusted to him. He had nothing good to show for the talent that he had been trusted with, and as a result he incurred the wrath of his master when he returned.

We might not all be able to achieve the same results, as we all have different abilities. However, whatever ability we do have can be used to do our best, whether we have five talents or one. That will bring the master's reward and approval. He wants us to do the best we can and be the best we can be. Our standard should be to do our very best with all our strength and ability— and with God's help. As Don Latham has noted: 'we were created to work, and the first priority is to do a good job.' After all, we are working for God and He deserves it. But it is a choice we make—moment by moment, and every day of our working life. It will require 'quiet champions', people who choose to do things God's way and to His standard, even when there seems to be little to be gained from doing it His way; and who keep choosing to press on with living a working life that is pleasing and glorifying to Him. The Bible encourages us to work hard and avoid laziness:

Lazy hands make a man poor, but diligent hands bring wealth.
Proverbs 10:4

Diligence will bring a reward because it is what God likes to see. He is not looking for a life that is out of balance, where work is an all consuming motivation, but a working life where we consistently do the best we can do, and be the best we can be. Some people at work are lazy. Some lazy people think their laziness is not being noticed, but sooner or later it will be. Some people are lazy because they think they will just get the same reward whether they work hard or not. But if our efforts are contingent upon the reward and recognition we get, then we will find lots of reasons for not giving our best. As Christians, the key is to know who we are serving through our work. If we do our work for the Lord, then we will be able and willing to maintain an excellent standard, whether we get recognition from people or whether we get nothing. That is the key that the kind of organisations described by Peters and Waterman are searching for—people's hearts and minds.

Giving our best is not just about diligence and effort. It is also about the kind of person we are in our everyday work environment. To give an example, Daniel showed diligence in his work, but also showed integrity in all that he did. When the king saw Daniel's excellent qualities as an administrator, he planned to make him administrator over the whole kingdom. Daniel's colleagues were jealous of the favour he was winning and tried to find something against him to bring him down. However, they could find no charge against him in the conduct of government affairs, 'because he was trustworthy and neither corrupt nor negligent' (Daniel 6:4).

KEEPING YOUR STANDARD HIGH

Now for the tough part. When you establish *excellence* as your work standard, there will be pressure for you to compromise. People, events, circumstances, and your own weaknesses can hinder your efforts to maintain a standard of excellence. There may be times when maintaining it does not seem to be worth the effort, and it may even cause problems for you. Part of the challenge facing Christians in the workplace is to be strong and rise above the common standard, relying on God to help us to maintain His standard. We will not be able to do it without His help!

We will probably find that at least some of our colleagues will not share the same commitment to giving their best. Nehemiah, for example, found that as he and the people were rebuilding the walls of Jerusalem, not everyone was prepared to make the same effort:

> The next section was repaired by the men of Tekoa, but their nobles would not put their shoulders to the work under their supervisors.
>
> *Nehemiah 3:5*

Nehemiah also found that hardened and devious people came along to mock, threaten and intimidate the workers, in an attempt to discourage them from completing the rebuilding work. As we have seen, Daniel also became the target of colleagues who were jealous of his success. When the colleagues could not find any evidence of corruption or negligence, they got the king to pass a law preventing people from praying to any god other than the king. This was designed to trap Daniel, as they knew he prayed to God. When Daniel was charged with the offence of praying to God, the king had no choice but to have him thrown into the lions' den.

The deviousness and destructiveness of people can sometimes be breathtaking. However, both Daniel and Nehemiah maintained their commitment to completing their work in a godly way.

It is not easy to keep your standard high. Here are some of the things that can discourage us from maintaining a standard of excellence and from giving our very best:

'Favourite sons and daughters'
Sometimes we can find ourselves in a situation where the boss favours others over us—but for reasons other than the quality or quantity of their work. Cliques and alliances can form, particularly if it is the sort of organisation where people generally stay for a long time. This can create undercurrents of loyalty to those in the clique, or exclusion for those outside it.

We can seem to miss out on a promotion opportunity despite our good and hard work. We may even work harder and better than those who are promoted, and a sense of resentment can take root in our heart when we seem to suffer injustice.

'But what thanks do you get?'

Lack of respect and recognition from our boss for our hard work, efforts and achievements can be demoralising.

'Snakes in the grass'

Our boss or colleagues can feel threatened by our good work, abilities, success, profile or achievements. This can lead them to try to make life difficult for us, and to withdraw their support when we need it. A threatened colleague is a dangerous colleague, who may well look for opportunities to undermine us and tarnish our reputation behind our back.

'It's just the way things are around here'

Custom and practice in the company, department or team can influence us if we are not watchful. The company culture could, for example, reflect an attitude that dishonesty is acceptable. Dishonesty such as overcharging the client, making shoddy goods and providing poor services can be rationalised away as 'not so bad', as 'just the way things work around here', or as 'just the way things work in this trade'. There can be an expectation, or even pressure, that we will do the same.

Research has shown that many people work in a culture of dishonesty. The results of a survey of 800 managers in the UK conducted by KPMG Forensic Accounting, *The Business of Ethics*, revealed that whilst 50% of managers were aware of fraudulent activities at work, some 40% turned a blind eye. Two thirds of the sample also agreed that everybody lies to the boss at some time.

'Oh, I can't wait to get out of this place'

The general morale of the organisation or office may be low, and the general attitudes and office conversation can pull down our own sense of morale or desire to achieve excellence.

'Glory grabbing'

Others stealing the credit for our work can discourage us from giving our best. In a large corporation where I was employed, the Chairman took a personal interest in a piece of work I was doing. When it came to presenting the work to a group of senior managers, my boss insisted on doing the presentation himself. He clearly saw an opportunity for some glory for himself. We went into a large boardroom and my boss presented the work. He was oblivious to the fact that he had just left me standing at the side without even introducing me to the meeting, and without letting me make any contribution. The work was not acknowledged as mine, and at the end of the presentation I was left to slip out of the room quietly while he stayed. It was not a good day. It is hard to respect a boss who seems to take the credit and seems to think that is entirely legitimate and justifiable. It is hard to carry on doing your best, but we have to remember who it is we are serving through our work.

To maintain our standards in the face of all the pressures and temptations to compromise requires us to be champions. We need to be people who will draw upon the grace of God to be overcomers in our circumstances—people who will set our faces like flint against the ways of the world, and choose to persevere in working and living God's way; people who will be strong in the things of God.

Here are some practical steps you can take, to help ensure that you keep your standard high despite everything:

Walk with the Lord
Maintain a close daily walk with the Lord, spending regular quality time with Him, and with the word of God. This will help ensure your mind and heart are renewed and the things of the day are kept in their right perspective. It will also help equip you with the wisdom you need to deal with the circumstances and people you face, and will build you up on the inside to give you the inner strength to cope with whatever life throws at you during the working day. Brother Lawrence discovered that peace and joy in his daily work came as he spent time in God's presence, turning to Him for the grace and help that he needed.

Forgive, forgive, forgive
Actively forgive your enemies and demonstrate forgiveness, and show a desire for reconciliation in your behaviour. This will give your enemies and the devil no opportunity to bring you down. If you seek to take revenge on others, or bear grudges, it will wear

you down, and it will give the enemy an opening to bring further trouble your way. I recently heard that a colleague who had damaged my reputation had been sacked for defrauding the company. The news came as a shock to everybody, as he had been there for over twenty years. He had taken a dislike to me and had tried to undermine me. The same night that I heard the news of his sacking, someone in my home-group felt led to read the following verses, not knowing anything of the events of my day:

> My tongue will tell of your righteous acts all day long, for those who wanted to harm me have been put to shame and confusion.
>
> *Psalm 71:24*

Do not get sucked into conflict with people who choose to be your enemy—the Lord will deal with them in His time and in His way.

On guard

Be wise and alert to the schemes that people undertake against you, asking the Holy Spirit to give you discernment about the motives and hearts of others. You need to be wise to what agendas other people may have against you. This will help you to be prudent in the way you work with people who have plans to harm you. Of course, we do meet some genuine people at work, but I have also found that some of the people who have been most friendly and helpful to me have been trying to undermine me because they wanted something I had—like my job. Friendliness can open us up, and when we are open we tend to give away useful information.

This is not to say we should not respond to friendliness, but we need to be careful to discern people's hearts, and ask God to open our eyes.

Remember who you are serving

Have a purpose in your heart to work ultimately to please God through your work, and not people. KEEP REMINDING YOURSELF! When you get this right in your mind, you will not depend upon praise or recognition from people in order to give your best, and you will not be so discouraged or disappointed when people let you down. You need to know who it is you are serving. A friend of myself and my wife recently returned from ten years of hard and dedicated missions work in South America. At the end of the ten years, the mother church handed the missions church over to a pastor who did not seem to be quite right spiritually and, when our friend returned home, the mother church seemed unsympathetic to her needs. She was hurt, but in the midst of her disappointment and heartbreak she said, 'You have to know who you are serving.' A lesson for us all.

Help!

Seek support and guidance from the Lord, and from Christian friends and leaders. Most of the problems you face at work are likely to have been experienced by others, and there will probably be someone in your church who has already faced the problem that you are facing—you just have to find them.

The power we need

Pray against spiritual opposition, and ask the Lord to help you. Prayer support from others can also be invaluable in helping you pull through a particular difficulty or problem at work. We also need to uphold each other in this way. When Nehemiah experienced opposition, he prayed:

> They were all trying to frighten us, thinking, "Their hands will get too weak for the work, and it will not be completed." But I prayed, "Now strengthen my hands."
>
> *Nehemiah 6:9*

How often in our churches do we specifically pray for working people? For healing, missions, finances—yes; but for people to see the power of God manifest in the workplace? —probably not very often, if ever.

We shall stand

Be strong in the face of opposition, and make an appropriate 'stand'—with wisdom and tact—at the right time, and in the right way, against wickedness, oppression, evil or the temptation or pressure to compromise. It is important to commit all struggles, burdens and battles to the Lord for His help. When Nehemiah faced lies from those who tried to intimidate him in his work, he spoke the truth straight back to them. (See Nehemiah 6:5–8.)

Guard your heart.
Learn to trust in the faithfulness and justice of God, and the truth of his word. The word of God can be a great comfort when we face opposition from others:

> The wicked draw the sword and bend the bow to bring down the poor and needy, to slay those whose ways are upright. But their swords will pierce their own hearts, and their bows will be broken.
> *Psalm 37:14–15*

God's word can be a great help when we face injustice or disappointment:

> Surely God is my help; the Lord is the one who sustains me.
> *Psalm 54:4*

If our mission statement is to work to God's standard of excellence in all that we do, then we have accepted a tough challenge. But it is possible, with His help, though we will need His grace every step of the way.

SUMMARY OF KEY POINTS

1. Give your best effort, and work to a standard of excellence. This is the pattern and standard established by God for us all to follow. However, this does not mean over-working or striving to achieve some unattainable standard of perfection. It means consistently doing your best in every way and at all times, with God's help.

2. Working to such a pattern and standard will be a challenge for us all. Other people we work with may have different standards and they, as well as the devil, will seek to discourage us from glorifying God through our work.

3. With God's help, and with our own determination, we **can** overcome all pressure to compromise our standards, and we can consistently do work that glorifies Him.

QUESTIONS FOR REFLECTION/DISCUSSION

1. In terms of the work you do in your workplace, what does (or should) 'excellence' look like?

2. Read Matthew 25:14–30. What lessons can we learn from the parable of the talents, in terms of the quality of work that God expects from us?

3. In Daniel 6:4, we read about how Daniel worked to a consistently high standard. From your experience, what tend to be the circumstances or events that distract or discourage people from consistently doing the best they can or from being the best they can be?

4. Think about someone you know who seems to be able to get other people to work to a good standard. What are the specific things he/she does or says that seem to get others to perform well?

5. Think about someone you know who seems to have a negative impact on the work or performance of others. What specific things does he/she say or do that seem to have such a negative impact?

6. A mission statement summarises the overall aim and standard of work that the organisation aspires to produce—basically, what it is in business to do. In terms of your own working life, what is your 'mission statement'?

7. Does the employer you work for have a mission statement? If not, what do you think it should say? If your employer does have a mission statement, then what notice do you think people take of it?

8. As Christians, what do you think should be the source of our motivation to work to an excellent standard?

9. What advice would you give a friend just starting his or her first job, to help them maintain a standard of excellence throughout their working life?

10. List ways in which anything from this chapter or from your review of the questions applies to you as a working person. Then list any **actions** you will take as a result of this study (e.g. further study or reflection, prayer, speaking to someone, requests for help, changing something about yourself) and be as specific as possible about **when** you will complete the action(s).

6

SO WHO ARE YOU AT WORK?

I recently did an exercise as part of a management development programme. My boss and the people who work for me completed a questionnaire to describe how they saw me as a manager. Some of the ratings and comments were a pleasant surprise, and provided confirmation of how I think I come across to other people. That was the good news. However, some of the ratings and comments showed areas where I needed to improve, highlighted things about me that I was not so aware of, and pointed to some of the things that seemed to have a surprisingly big impact on other people.

What we say and do at work does have a big impact on people, though we may not always realise it. We can have a positive impact on their sense of self-worth, motivation and performance, but we can also have an equally powerful but negative impact. Comments, gestures and the tone of our voice can communicate what we really think about people much more than what we actually say. But sometimes we are not aware of the impact we do have. We can have blind spots (where others are aware of our weaknesses, but we are not) and we can be so busy that we are insensitive to the impact of our comments and behaviour on the other person.

The sort of people we are—and particularly the way we deal

with others—will affect how successful we are in our work. It will also affect our Christian witness. As Charles Swindoll has observed, what demonstrates our faith is our behaviour at work, not how we behave on Sunday morning. When we are in church, it is easy to look friendly, patient, loving, kind, and helpful with other people. It is also relatively easy to say the 'right' things in the church context, such as blessing someone we hardly know as we shake hands. These things can, of course, be genuine. However, there can be differences between the kind of picture we project to others, for example at church, and who we really are when we are at work, where none of our Christian friends or leaders can see us, and where the expectations and pressures are different.

But what sort of person should one be at work? I remember struggling with this question for the first few years of my working life. I had many questions, such as: should I be involved socially with work colleagues or keep myself completely separate? Should I be tough with people, or 'soft' and caring? Should I project myself confidently, or let others take the higher profile? Should I stand up and challenge people, or turn the other cheek when they seem to do something against my best interests, or to harm me? If I suffer some injustice from the boss, should I just submit—or is it acceptable for Christians to challenge the boss? Is it right to be ambitious—or should I be content with what I have? It seemed to be difficult to find any guidance on these matters.

The answer to these questions, is, of course, to be Christ-like at all times, and the only way to be Christ-like is to be filled with Christ on the inside then see him reflected on the outside in who we are and how we behave. The only way we can consistently be Christ-like is to be transformed on the inside first—in our values, attitudes of the heart, and character. The Holy Spirit can help us by opening our eyes to see where we need to change, and he can bring about that change. Christ will then be reflected on the outside, in the things we do and say as well as the way we work. As Steve Walton has written, 'Christian people need to be those who live out the faith they profess in their daily lives. If we do that, we will stand out as distinctive people who show compassion, mercy and patience, as those who treat the marginalised of our society with the love which God Himself has for them.... But God's call is a call to live distinctively, to let our lights shine in a dark world.'[1] If we try to put on a 'front' of being considerate and caring, the chances are that sooner or later people will see through it, if it is not genuine. People have a habit of getting to the truth about who we are. They can spot our weaknesses when we spend a lot of time with them. They will test us, and try to discern what we are really like behind what we choose to show them. Unless it is real it will not work.

But what does 'being Christ-like' look like in terms of who we are at work? This is the type of behaviour we would expect to see, with Christ as the standard or model for who we are at work:

PEOPLE WITH ASSURANCE

When the Lord appeared to Moses through the burning bush and called him to go to Egypt to bring His people from captivity and take them to the promised land, Moses was far from assured about his ability to do the job. His initial response was:

'Who am I, that I should go to Pharaoh and bring the Israelites out of Egypt?'

Exodus 3:11

He worried about whether the people would believe him or listen to him if he did go to them, and he pointed out that he was far from eloquent as a speaker. God dealt with his lack of assurance. He encouraged him to see that He Himself was sending him. It was a God-given task to be done. God assured him that He would demonstrate His power to the Egyptians and, as a result, they would let the people go; God gave Moses a foretaste of this power by turning his staff into a snake, and making his hand leprous. The Lord assured him that He would help Moses every step of the way:

'Now go; I will help you speak and will teach you what to say.'

Exodus 4:12

---

[1] S. Walton, *A Call to live: Vocation for Everyone*, Triangle 1994. Used by permission of SPCK

God encouraged him to go and demonstrate the power He had given him. When the Lord called Joshua to complete the job that Moses had started, He put deep assurance into him, which he needed in order to fulfil the task of leading the people into the promised land. Several times, He told Joshua to 'be strong and courageous' (Joshua 1:6). God promised him that He would give him every place where he set his foot; and that if he followed God he would have victory after victory, and would prosper. God also assured him that he would not be alone in fulfilling the job:

> 'No one will be able to stand up against you all the days of your life. As I was with Moses, so I will be with you; I will never leave you nor forsake you.'
>
> *Joshua 1:5*

He gave him emotional reassurance and told him not to be terrified or discouraged by the scale of the task, nor by the struggles and difficulties he would face along the way.

In the New Testament, we note that Jesus only spoke positive things about himself. He knew who he was, what he had to do, and where he was going. He knew what the Father had set before him to do. Confidently and boldly, he did the Father's will in all things. We need to have assurance—both about our standing before God, and our particular calling at work. Christian assurance of salvation is a gift of God; the assurance that we are doing the Father's will is based on faithful obedience to His word and responsiveness to the Holy Spirit. If we lack appropriate assurance, we will be abused, exploited and kicked around in the workplace. Is that what God wants to see? I do not think so.

God's champions in the workplace need to have the assurance that Moses and Joshua received. Not arrogance, that comes from pride in our own abilities, but a confidence that comes from knowing who we are in God—from knowing that what we are doing is a godly enterprise; and from a steadfast faith that God will be with us and will help us. We are called to do a job. It may not be leading a whole nation, but whatever we are given to do, if we choose to do it God's way, it will be a challenge. We need the assurance that comes from knowing that He has called us, will equip us, help us, and fight the battles for us. We need to have the confidence that comes from knowing that He will fulfil

His plan through us if we walk in obedience with Him. To see our workplaces transformed for God will require us to be strong and very courageous, just like Joshua. What assurance we can have when, in our hearts, we know that God has called us to do what we are doing! He will be right there with us to see it through. We need the assurance that we are God's champions. As Edwin Cole has correctly observed, 'to become a champion, you must see yourself as a champion.' If we have no confidence from knowing who we are in God, then we are unlikely to have the courage and strength to press on through difficulties, to face the challenges of the workplace head on, and to overcome. An advertisement designed to attract people to join the military in a South East Asian nation read as follows: 'Tough times will come and go. Tough people don't.' We need the inner assurance to be over-comers in the workplace.

WISE, NOT NAIVE

While, as Christians, we are to show qualities such as love, peace, patience and forgiveness, we must also be able to discern good from evil and truth from falsehood. People at work can be good at concealing their motives, and sometimes want to harm us rather than to help us. Hatred, jealousy, strife, competition and revenge can motivate those around us to seek ways to harm us and drive us away, though it may be hidden by superficial friendliness. When Jesus sent out the twelve disciples, he said:

> 'I am sending you out like sheep among wolves. Therefore be as shrewd as snakes and as innocent as doves.'
>
> *Matthew 10:16*

Have you ever been surprised to find that someone you thought was an ally has really been an enemy all along? I have. We will need to be as shrewd as snakes to discern the motives and tactics of other people if we are going to deal with them and work with them effectively, and if we are not going to fall into the traps that they may try to set for us. James encourages us to ask God for wisdom:

> If any of you lacks wisdom, he should ask God, who gives
> generously to all without finding fault, and it will be given to him.
>
> *James 1:5*

We need to turn to the Lord and His word for wisdom, help
and discernment. The Holy Spirit is our counsellor, who will lead
us into all truth. We need to ask him to open our eyes to discern
truth from falsehood, so that we can see the real motives behind
what people do and say.

If we are going to thrive in the working world, and do things
God's way, we will need to stand firm and be bold and courageous
in our dealings with others. We will need to be prepared to tackle
the difficult—and often messy—issues. An area where many
working people with management responsibility struggle is
dealing with poor performing staff. It can be easier to ignore the
fact that someone is under performing, taking excessive sick leave
or wasting time, rather than to confront them and deal with the
problem firmly but fairly. If we are called to manage resources
as good stewards for God, then we have a responsibility to deal
with such issues wisely, effectively and in a timely way. People
and time are resources, as well as materials and money. If you do
not know how to deal with such issues, then there will be courses
you can take, or colleagues who can advise you. It is important
to be properly equipped to tackle the 'people management'
issues, because if they are badly handled things can be made
much worse.

HONEST AND FAITHFUL

God is looking for honesty and faithfulness from His workplace
'champions'. When the Lord laid out for His people the
guidelines and laws for how to live a holy life, He instructed them
to be honest in their commercial affairs:

> Do not use dishonest standards when measuring length, weight or
> quantity. Use honest scales and honest weights, an honest ephah
> and an honest hin.
>
> *Leviticus 19:35–36*

Such honesty really matters to God. We read in Proverbs that:

SO WHO ARE YOU AT WORK?

> The LORD abhors dishonest scales,
> but accurate weights are his delight.
>
> *Proverbs 11:1*

Honesty will be noticed. Dishonesty will also be noticed. For example, when Joash was king, the money that was brought to the temple was handled by honest people, who gave it to the workmen—who used it to make repairs to the place of worship. We read that the people who handled the money were not required to give an account as to how the money was used 'because they acted with complete honesty' (2 Kings 12:15). Their honesty was well known, and as a result they were trusted.

In the workplace we need to be honest in how we handle the resources that have been entrusted to us. This includes the time, money and materials that belong to the company. We also need to be honest in all our dealings with people, including employees and customers. If we lie to an employee, or if we are inconsistent with people, it will usually be a matter of time before we are discovered. It will be difficult to win the trust of people after that, and our Christian witness will be damaged. There will certainly be opportunities to be dishonest at work. Take, for example, the writing of résumés or CVs. Recent research has shown that three out of four CVs from job applicants have been embellished —that is, the truth has been distorted—and a third of CVs contain outright lies as an attempt to show the applicant in a good light. In reality, of course, a distortion of the truth is also a lie. It may be common, but that does not make it right.

PEOPLE WHO VALUE PEOPLE

The kind of person you are at work will be strongly influenced by the value you place on other people. We read about the centurion who valued his servant:

> ...a centurion's servant, whom his master valued highly, was sick and about to die.
>
> *Luke 7:2*

Because the centurion valued his servant, he sought help from Jesus to heal him. Though he was a powerful man, he took the trouble to help a lowly servant. His faith amazed the Lord, and his servant was healed. Had the centurion not valued the servant for who he was in the first place, he could easily have seen his illness as an inconvenience; and his actions as well as the outcome might well have been different. He cared, and because he cared, he did something visible and meaningful to help.

In many companies, the corporate literature refers to employees as their greatest or most important asset, but the employment experience of the workforce can suggest that the reality is quite different. There may be a wide gap between the corporate values and the way people actually behave. The employee–employer relationship should, however, be a partnership based on mutual respect. That is the biblical model. In Ephesians, we read that slaves were encouraged to obey their masters with respect and fear, and with sincerity of heart, as if they were serving Christ. Masters were also urged: 'Treat your slaves in the same way' (6:9).

PEOPLE WHO ARE INVOLVED

Building good quality relationships with people, without compromising our Christian principles, is one of the keys to an effective Christian witness. It is through our positive influence on the people around us that we can touch their lives and release the transforming power of the love of God. It is also through others that we can have an impact on the atmosphere and culture of the organisation we work for; and our relationships can be an engine for positive change. Not only that, but other people can have ideas, make suggestions and give us feedback that can be a very valuable source of data for identifying how we need to improve our approach to others and the way that we work. Unless we build relationships, it is unlikely that we will build effectively for the kingdom of God. But if we make the effort to build constructive and collaborative relationships with the people around us, we can reach the workplace mission field, and we can let our light shine before men, '...that they may see your good deeds and praise your Father in heaven' (Matthew 5:16).

It is relatively easy to keep ourselves separate from people in our day to day working life. It is also relatively easy to be involved with people and at the same time be unholy. It is not so easy both to be involved with the people around us and to remain holy. However, that is the challenge for us.

Jesus was involved with people. Jesus was himself God's love made flesh so that he could be more intimately and visibly involved in our lives. He mixed with sinners, yet he remained holy. He was invited to dinner at the house of a Pharisee, and accepted the invitation. Not only that, but there was a woman there who had lived a sinful life, and everybody knew it. However, Jesus allowed her to wet his feet with her tears, dry his feet with her hair, and pour perfume over him! He allowed her to get close to him; he drew close to people.

The people Jesus mixed with might not be the sort of people with whom we would naturally wish to associate—but something very good came from his encounter with the woman. Jesus used the occasion to forgive her sins, and to teach the Pharisee and other guests about the power of mercy and forgiveness.

FAIR AND JUST

The word of God encourages us to treat others with fairness, justice and sincerity. To take advantage of those who are less powerful or more vulnerable than us; to show discrimination, or to practise exploitation, is to fall short of the mark of a champion.

Before the people of Israel entered the promised land, the Lord reminded them of the Law, in order to prepare them. Part of this teaching related to the fair and just treatment of employees:

> Do not take advantage of a hired man who is poor and needy, whether he is a brother Israelite or an alien living in one of your towns. Pay him his wages each day before sunset, because he is poor and is counting on it.
>
> *Deuteronomy 24:14–15*

We should pay and reward people according to what they deserve and according to what we have agreed is the rate of pay. Besides paying them what they deserve, we should also seek to give them the credit for the work they have done, rather than take the credit and recognition for their achievement or hard work. Not only is this pleasing to God, it sows something positive into the lives of others; it will encourage them, and provide a positive role model for them to follow. Sooner or later, people make a connection between our behaviour and our faith. If the people we work with find that we deal with things fairly, they will see in us something of the God we worship.

Fairness and justice go far beyond simply paying people appropriately and recognising their work. When these values are allowed to permeate the culture of the organisation, even through our small efforts and influence, they can profoundly influence every aspect of working life, ensuring people are treated with dignity and respect.

LOVING AND FORGIVING

Most of us cannot choose whom we work with. We find ourselves rubbing shoulders with all kinds of people: some friendly, some not so friendly; some we like, some we do not; some who like us, and some who do not like us. There will be people who unknowingly wrong us, hinder us or harm us in some way. There will also be others who knowingly do so, and even take pleasure in it. The temptation is always to retaliate, either directly by harming them back, or indirectly by maligning them with our friends at work—to discredit or undermine them, or to minimise them as a threat. Our response can also be to avoid the person. At least if we keep out of their way, we can keep our anger and vengeful feelings towards the person at bay. However, retaliation and avoidance are not the mark of love. In contrast, this is what love is about:

> Love is patient, love is kind. It does not envy, it does not boast, it is not proud. It is not rude, it is not self-seeking, it is not easily angered, it keeps no record of wrongs. Love does not delight in evil, but rejoices with the truth. It always protects, always trusts, always hopes, always perseveres. Love never fails....
>
> *1 Corinthians 13:4–8*

The word of God encourages us to get rid of all slander and malice from our lives. When Paul wrote to the Colossians, he urged them to, 'rid yourselves of all such things as these: anger, rage, malice, slander and filthy language from your lips' (Colossians 3:8). Similarly, when Peter wrote to encourage Christians to live holy lives, he urged them to: 'rid yourselves of all malice and all deceit, hypocrisy, envy and slander of every kind' (1 Peter 2:1). But it goes further than just getting ourselves right. We are also called to be a blessing to our enemies, to fight evil with good, and to be righteous when faced with the temptation to sin. We are called to return something positive to someone who has chosen to be our enemy, and to make every effort to build a good relationship with them. In short, we are called to put love into action, as Jesus said:

> 'You have heard that it was said, "Love your neighbour and hate your enemy." But I tell you: Love your enemies and pray for those who persecute you, that you may be sons of your Father in heaven.'
> *Matthew 5:43–45*

The hallmark of a champion is to love our enemies. If we bear grudges and get drawn into disputes, factions and fights with those who come against us, we are likely to get hurt, and our Christian witness will be destroyed. Not only that, but the quality of our work performance and that of our colleagues is likely to fall as the level of co-operation, collaboration and trust falls. Hence, forgiveness can have an impact on the 'bottom line' of the company. Forgiveness has been aptly described as functioning rather similarly to the oil in an engine. It is essential to its proper operation. If there is unforgiveness, much damage is done, in all kinds of ways, to individuals and organizations. Forgiveness is both the Lord's command to us and necessary for human beings to work together effectively.

CHRIST'S AMBASSADORS

We are ambassadors, or representatives, of Jesus Christ in the workplace, called to manifest his love and his character to those around us, in all the practicalities of our working day. If, in all the ways we work, react to events, and relate to people, we show the reality of Christ, then God will draw people to Himself. If there is something good about us which people find attractive, some aspect of us that they value, then they will come to see that

God is real in our lives. We are a prophetic people, through whom God can speak to the lost—using us as we are.

> We are therefore Christ's ambassadors, as though God were making his appeal through us.
>
> *2 Corinthians 5:20*

The qualities of Jesus Christ will stand out in the workplace because they are so fundamentally different from the ways of the world. If we show the fruit of the Spirit in our workplace, this will surely get noticed, for:

> ...the fruit of the Spirit is love, joy, peace, patience, kindness, goodness, faithfulness, gentleness and self-control.
>
> *Galatians 5:22–23*

When we demonstrate these qualities consistently, in the moment by moment practical details of the working day, what a profound effect we will have on others' lives, as well as on the culture and atmosphere of the place where we work.

Being Christ-like is not about working harder and harder to change ourselves to be a 'Christ-like looking person', it is about being filled with the Spirit of Jesus, being transformed by him, yielding to that transforming work, and allowing him to change us.

SUMMARY OF KEY POINTS

1. It matters to God who we really are at work, not who we think we are, nor the 'person' we may try to project to others. Who we really are will affect how successful we are in our work, and will have an impact on the effectiveness of our Christian witness. Our work colleagues are usually good at seeing through any pretence or 'front'.

2. The word of God provides a useful mirror for us. When we look into it, it will show us what we are really like, rather than what, perhaps, we would like to see.

3. A clear picture of who we really are at work is the best starting point for positive change. We can then ask the Lord to transform us, so that we manifest Him in all the things we do at work, and in all the interactions and working relationships we have with others. Let us ask the Lord to work in us, so that more of Him is manifested as a shining light to a dark world!

QUESTIONS FOR REFLECTION/DISCUSSION

1. From your experience, what tend to be the main differences between the way the company or employer says its employees should behave and the way people actually behave at work?

2. What are some of the circumstances at work where you perceive what someone is really like, rather than what they would like you to see? Can you think of some examples?

3. What type of behaviour and attitudes would you associate with someone being an effective 'ambassador for Christ' in the workplace?

4. Carefully consider the qualities outlined in Galatians 5:22–23. What would these qualities look like in terms of behaviour at work?

5. How can you show in practical ways that you value someone at work?

6. Is there any pressure or opportunity to be dishonest at work? How do people usually respond?

7. Do you think it is good for Christians to be confident about our own abilities?

8. When Jesus sent out his disciples, he said they should be as shrewd as snakes and as innocent as doves. How do you think this applies to us in the workplace?

9. Write down a list of words that you think best describe the sort of person you are at work. Which words do you think your colleagues would use to describe you?

10. List the ways in which anything from this chapter or your review of the above questions applies to you as a working person in your circumstances. Then list any **actions** you will take as a result of this study (e.g. further study or reflection, prayer, speaking to someone, requests for help, changing something about yourself) and be as specific as possible about **when** you will complete the action(s).

7

MAKING WORKING
RELATIONSHIPS WORK

In many ways, our relationships, rather than the work itself, can be the most difficult and challenging aspect of working life. Listen to people when they complain or grumble at work. More often than not it is some aspect of inter-personal communication or relationships that is causing them concern. Just think about when you get annoyed at work. How often is it because of something to do with relationships, rather than the work itself? Working relationships can be fun, supportive and satisfying. However, they can also be messy, unpleasant, demanding and downright frustrating. At their worst, working relationships can be destructive and damaging. Employment tribunal cases against employers on the grounds of race and sex discrimination, for example, indicate that all is not well in the British workplace, and there is a similar story to tell in workplaces everywhere. British Home Office figures indicate that during one year alone some twenty nine tribunal cases against the Metropolitan Police were settled out of court, at a cost of more than half a million pounds. Cases of people who have suffered years of abuse in the workplace are not uncommon.

Whilst not many of us will suffer extreme forms of abuse or discrimination, we can all experience difficulties in our working relationships from time to time. Most of us will be working under the authority of someone else, but that someone may not be our ideal boss. Rather than protect us, develop us and provide the direction and resources we need, our boss may at times seem to make life difficult for us. In most jobs we work with other people; some are our colleagues, while others may report to us. In many ways, they are also unlikely to be our ideal colleagues or subordinates. However, it is uncomfortable to think that we may not be their ideal subordinate, colleague or boss either! If the spotlight of the Holy Spirit shone on your working relationships now, what would he find?

Working relationships can, of course be good, but they can also be coloured or dominated by all kinds of tensions, underlying 'agendas', difficulties, conflicts, misunderstandings, malice, and 'office politics'. Some people can be devious, malicious, unjust and insensitive towards us for no obvious reason. We can come across people who try to work out their plan to harm us, over a long period of time and little by little, so that we may not even notice what is going on unless we are alert and discerning. The devil can also be at work trying to harm us through our relationships with other people. He loves to stir people to come against us, to try to defeat us, and to destroy our Christian witness in the workplace. He will try to disarm and defeat God's champions. In the workplace, the general conversation can be dominated by everyone discussing their frustrations with other people, or with the way the organisation works, and alliances and factions can be based on a common 'enemy', such as the boss or an unpopular colleague. This pulls morale down, creating a destructive atmosphere of mistrust. We can get frustrated, discouraged or even bitter by difficulties in working relationships, especially if there seems to be no way out for us. All this can be hurtful, discouraging and even damaging to us, and the impact can spill over into other areas of our life, affecting the quality of our work and our psychological, physical and spiritual well-being, as well as our relationships at home.

In the face of all this, we can be enormously frustrated by our working relationships. It can feel like the spiritual, physical and emotional strength within just gets sapped away by the daily niggles and hassles that are often part of working with others. Perhaps our perspective needs to change. Robert Mattox reminds us that, as Christians, we may not actually enjoy working with non-Christians, because they are not 'stamped with the same nature', and the pressures of secular office life 'combine to burst our spiritual bubble of peace and joy.'[1] There is, however, an alternative perspective for Christians. The quality of our relationships and our attitudes to other people in the workplace are important to God, and He wants us to see them as important too. Our challenge is not only to cultivate good quality relationships with boss, colleagues and subordinates, difficult though that may be, it is to go beyond just getting along with people—to move to a point where our relationships are a good influence, a channel of blessing, and a catalyst for positive change in the lives of those around us; a tough challenge indeed, particularly if we are not naturally outgoing.

If our working relationships are to be a force for good, and the yeast that will bring about positive change in the world around us, then we need to start with our heart. Whatever is on the inside, in terms of our attitudes and values, will be reflected outwardly in our behaviour and relationships. For example, when we pick out mistakes in the work of others it could be from a good motive, such as to achieve excellent results, and it may even be part of our job to do so. It could be done tactfully, in a way that is supportive to the person, and that builds their confidence, reflecting a heart attitude that people are important. On the other hand, we can do it for a whole range of other reasons, such as to demonstrate how clever we are, to make ourselves feel good, to reinforce our status difference, or to put the other person down. Correcting others can also reflect a desire to control them, to get revenge, or to feed our pride. The person on the receiving end is likely to be able to sense the motive behind our behaviour, even though we may think we are good at hiding it, and our relationship with them, as well as our Christian witness, will be affected.

So we need a heart that is changed by the Lord, a heart which is filled with the Lord, and a heart of flesh, not of stone. We need a heart that has a sense of compassion, and the ability to see life through the eyes of other people, a heart that forgives and

---

[1] In R. Mattox, *The Christian Employee*, Bridge, 1978

always seeks to build others up and to do them good. As Christians, we should honour our boss and try to work co-operatively and collaboratively with others, whether they are nice to us or not. We should take the first step to mend broken or strained relationships, whether it is our fault or not that there are difficulties. This is not to say that we should be 'soft' people who let others just walk all over us. Sometimes we will need to be robust enough to stand our ground, when people try to knock us down, manipulate and intimidate us, or take advantage of us. We should not let them do that. Sometimes we will need to guard our heart from wickedness and direct attack, and turn to the Lord for strength and healing for our hurts before we can carry on with the business of making working relationships work. Positive people with positive working relationships can have a positive impact wherever they are.

PEOPLE WITH A POSITIVE APPROACH
TO THE BOSS

For many people, the relationship with their boss can be a daily struggle, characterised by resentment, misunderstanding and mistrust. We can get upset when the boss makes a comment, does something badly, or takes a decision that we feel does not sufficiently take into account our feelings—or is just simply a bad decision. The result can be resentment, a breakdown of trust and a loss of respect for the person we report to. Much time can be wasted in the workplace, discussing the weaknesses and mistakes of the boss with colleagues, building up a shared understanding of what the boss is really like. Just below the surface of superficial politeness there can be undercurrents of hatred and rebellion. However, as Christians we are called to have an approach to the boss which is characterised by respect, submission, helpfulness, co-operation and trust, as well as a willingness and desire to benefit him or her by the way we work. As champions for God in the workplace, our challenge is to cultivate and sustain such a positive approach—whatever the boss is like towards us.

Peter encouraged Christians to see a greater purpose in the

sufferings that we can face, and this shows us how to live our life in the face of struggles and suffering in a way that glorifies God. He encouraged slaves to submit with respect to their masters, whether the masters treated them well or badly:

> Slaves, submit yourselves to your masters with all respect, not only to those who are good and considerate, but also to those who are harsh.
>
> *1 Peter 2:18*

Of course, in the modern context, our working relationship with our employer is not one of slave and master, and there is a raft of employment legislation that prevents an employer from abusing employees. However, Peter does capture the important principle that submission, respect and honour for the boss should not be conditional upon what he or she is like, nor upon what he or she does. If the boss is a poor manager who cannot be trusted, then we should have the same positive heart attitude and approach toward him as if he were an excellent boss.

> Serve wholeheartedly, as if you were serving the Lord, not men.
>
> *Ephesians 6:7*

God has established the authorities over us, including our boss, and our life should reflect a respect for God-ordained authority—whether they are godly people or not. The power and effectiveness of our Christian witness will depend, to a large extent, upon the way we show respect, faithful service, submission and trustworthiness towards our boss.

Paul outlined to Titus various principles that should be taught in the church, pointing to the need to teach people how to relate to their master in a way that gives a good Christian witness:

> Teach slaves to be subject to their masters in everything, to try to please them, not to talk back to them, and not to steal from them, but to show that they can be fully trusted, so that in every way they will make the teaching about God our Saviour attractive.
>
> *Titus 2:9–10*

If we show we can be fully trusted, and that we respect and honour the boss, it will certainly be noticed—and these are qualities that any boss will value. However, if someone is a lazy and inefficient employee, it will irritate and anger the boss, 'as vinegar to the teeth and smoke to the eyes' (Proverbs 10:26). If we are willing followers, who resist the urge to complain and argue, we will be a joy to work with, and we will shine out as different, very different:

> Do everything without complaining or arguing, so that you may become blameless and pure, children of God without fault in a crooked and depraved generation, in which you shine like stars in the universe.
>
> *Philippians 2:14–15*

Our approach should be to serve the boss in a way that aims to benefit him or her. Rather than our interests and agenda being the driving force, it should be the interests of the boss that shape our goals and actions. When Abraham's chief servant asked God to help him to find a wife for Isaac at Abraham's request, his motive was that his master would be pleased. He wanted God to help him be successful in his task, so that Abraham and his family would be blessed. Our daily question should be: what can I do to help my boss, to make his/ her job easier, to improve the boss's position, success, status, and confidence? Our daily prayer as we go to work should be 'Lord give me success today so that my boss, and this organisation, will be blessed and prosper.'

As we saw earlier, the servants who used their talents conscientiously and proactively to increase the wealth of the master were rewarded and favoured, whereas the servant who brought no benefit with his talent was rejected as worthless. If we are to do what the boss wants, we must listen to what the boss wants. We may need to ask questions to be absolutely clear what he or she requires from us. Many problems in working relationships arise from ineffective communication. A few questions can be a great help, bringing clarity and shared understanding. Try asking some questions to clarify where the boss sees things going, or to ascertain the improvements you should make to the way you work and to your performance. If you are not sure what you should be doing, or you are sitting there frustrated because you do not know what the priorities are, try asking for clarity (but without implying that the manager is not doing his or her job!) Similarly, if you ask someone to do some work for you, make sure you have a shared understanding about what has to be done, how you want them to do it, and by when. Just as you cannot read his mind when it comes to understanding what your boss wants, your staff cannot read your mind either! The good and faithful servant (in Matthew chapter 25) knew exactly what the boss wanted to see from him. As a result, he successfully delivered what was required, gaining the reward he deserved.

During the course of our working day, there will be many opportunities for us to demonstrate whether we are loyal to those in positions of authority over us. There will be conversations among colleagues, for example, where we can be drawn into slandering or undermining the reputation and honour of the boss. ('You'll never guess what he said…. he thinks he's a really good manager, but do you know what he said to her the other day….she said, and then he said, and then she said….') One small comment or action by the boss can get analysed and discussed far and wide. This is not the sort of thing we should participate in.

There will also be occasions when we have the opportunity to harm the boss, or give less than our best efforts. The temptation to compromise our loyalty will be strongest when the boss has wronged us in some way. David provides a model of loyalty. Even though David had been anointed, Saul was still king—but a bad one; he was jealous of David, seeing him as a threat to his own position. Saul therefore sought to kill David, in order to keep his own position of power, and he ruthlessly pursued him. Some bosses can be like that, when they have talented staff under them, to protect their long-term positions. But despite Saul's malice, David honoured and respected his authority because he knew that his position had been God-ordained. He had an opportunity to kill Saul but did not do so. Instead, David sought to be humbly reconciled with him:

> "Why is my Lord pursuing his servant? What have I done, and what wrong am I guilty of?"
>
> *1 Samuel 26:18*

To cultivate and maintain such a positive relationship with the boss will require us to trust the Lord to work things out. David trusted the Lord, and eventually He removed Saul and established David in his rightful position as king. If the boss tries to block our progress, or do us harm, we need to believe that 'those who hope in the Lord will inherit the land' (Psalm 37:9). He will uphold us in our integrity if we seek to follow His principles. Even though evil people may seem to prosper for a while, the Lord will protect and prosper us, and those who abuse their authority will be judged—if not now, when the Lord returns to judge the living and the dead. There are many passages in the Psalms that encourage us to see how God will help and protect us, and deal with our enemies. Here are some to meditate upon:

> They spread a net for my feet—
> I was bowed down in distress.
> They dug a pit in my path—
> but they have fallen into it themselves.
>
> *Psalm 57:6*

> The LORD is my light and my salvation—
> whom shall I fear?
> The LORD is the stronghold of my life—
> of whom shall I be afraid?
> When evil men advance against me
> to devour my flesh,
> when my enemies and my foes attack me,
> they will stumble and fall.
>
> *Psalm 27:1–2*

> Do not fret because of evil men
> or be envious of those who do wrong;
> for like the grass they will soon wither,
> like green plants they will soon die away....
> Be still before the LORD and wait patiently for him;
> do not fret when men succeed in their ways,
> when they carry out their wicked schemes.
> Refrain from anger and turn from wrath;
> do not fret—it leads only to evil.
> For evil men will be cut off,
> but those who hope in the Lord will inherit the land.
>
> *Psalm 37:1, 7–9*

Whilst we will need to trust in the Lord to work things out, and whilst we are to honour and submit to those placed over us, there are also times when we can prayerfully take practical steps to deal with difficulties in our relationship with the boss—such as when we disagree. Disagreements may be for 'positive' reasons, such as having an idea about how to organise the work more efficiently or to do the work more effectively. Our idea may be good but we still need to share our ideas and suggestions in a constructive way, which demonstrates support and respect for our boss, rather than in a way which embarrasses or undermines him or her, even unintentionally. Make suggestions in a way which he or she is most likely to find acceptable ('You may have already thought of this, but….one thing you may wish to consider is…' or, 'I don't know what you will think about this as an idea but….'; 'I've had an idea, but see what you think….')

From time to time we can also become unhappy because of a more fundamental disagreement, conflict or grievance with the boss. Resolving such differences should be done constructively and respectfully. The more personal or sensitive matters should be dealt with privately, in a way which does not embarrass the boss, and in a way that is consistent with any company policies. To openly tell other colleagues about how we feel about something the boss has said or done to us can undermine the reputation of the boss and make the 'atmosphere' around the relationship worse. Our tone and approach to resolving conflicts with the person in authority over us—usually your line manager—is very important, and is likely to reflect our heart attitudes.

In such a situation, when it is necessary to confront an employer, it can be appropriate to start by saying that you value the job, and that your purpose is to help to sustain a good working relationship. Ensure that your words are constructive. Any such conversation should be the subject of prayer first. We also need to ensure that there is no malice in our heart before we confront a difficulty in a relationship. We need to bring it to the Lord first, and resolve it with Him before we bring it to the other person.

It can be useful to identify the source of any difficulties in a relationship and try to deal with the cause by taking practical steps to improve things. Difficulties can arise for many reasons. Sometimes we ourselves can be the cause of the difficulty. Even if we are not the cause of the problem we can still take steps, both practically and in prayer, to make things better and to be the cause of the solution. Possible sources of problems in our boss-subordinate relationship can include the following:

- ☐ Pride, and our unwillingness to accept correction, instructions or authority over us;
- ☐ Poor communication, leading to misunderstandings that are not resolved, as well as to mistrust;
- ☐ Inability or unwillingness of one 'side' to listen to the other 'side';
- ☐ The boss feeling threatened by our abilities, success and profile in the organisation;
- ☐ Our envy of the boss's position, status, benefits or authority;
- ☐ Strife, and self-seeking for credit;
- ☐ Pressure of work—leading to frustration or impatience with people;
- ☐ Lack of effective management skills or a conflict of management styles;
- ☐ The tendency for our respect and honour for the boss to depend upon his/her competence or performance;
- ☐ Not knowing each other well enough, including how the boss thinks, feels and works, as well as the expectations he/she has regarding us and our work;
- ☐ Mistakes or problems from the past dominating the current atmosphere;
- ☐ Anger or bitterness inside us in the face of injustice or mistreatment;
- ☐ Lack of basic work controls such as clarity about what work has to be done, by whom, by when and to what standard;
- ☐ An office culture where the boss's weaknesses are discussed, analysed and amplified behind his/her back, or where negative and sarcastic humour sets the tone.

One common cause of difficulties in working relationships is poor communication, or miscommunication, which can lead to misunderstandings that can all too easily lead to a breakdown in a relationship. Big fires start with small sparks, and big problems in relationships can start from one small comment or gesture. People can say things they do not really mean—it can just come out the wrong way. But before we react negatively to comments, it is good to stop and think—and ask for clarification from the other person if we are unsure as to what they mean.

Dealing with some of these issues may require us to repent, forgive, make a choice to love the other person, and take the first practical steps toward cultivating a more harmonious and positive relationship. Whilst we may feel that we are the victims of a bad boss, or of injustice, we, as Christians, should aim to take the first practical steps, praying for reconciliation—even if the problem is not our 'fault'. Applying God's principles to a difficult relationship can be a powerful witness, and an experience for us which will help us mature in our Christian life. Charles Swindoll points out that to have the right attitude can be especially hard if the person under whom you work is difficult, or an incompetent leader, and that this tests both our loyalty and Christian maturity.[1]

PEOPLE WITH A POSITIVE APPROACH TO COLLEAGUES AND WORKMATES

The people who work closest to us, including our colleagues, workmates and those who report to us or work for us, will get to know who we really are. During the course of the working day, and as they get to know us over time, they will see how we respond, how we relate—not just what we *say* we will do, but what we *actually* do in the face of all kinds of pressures and circumstances. If our Christian walk and witness is real, they will see it. If it is compromised or shallow, they will see it. We will be to them a representative of God. Whatever we are like, that is what they will come to think that our God is like. How we approach our colleagues matters.

If we are prepared to mix with people, then opportunities will open up to bring some good into people's lives. If we go to lunch with our colleagues, sooner or later all kinds of issues will surface. They will open up about their financial struggles, their

---

[1] In *A Man of Integrity and Forgiveness: Joseph*, Word Publishing, 1998

frustrations with their spouse, the hurt, disappointment and bitterness they feel from their broken marriage, or their sense of failure at who they are or where they are in life. It may come across thinly disguised in their jokes, but we will come face to face with what is really going on. They might resent our joy, and the blessing of God in our life, and that might all come out too. But these are open doors for Christians to show concern, to show tactfully how we see things differently and how we respond differently to the problems we face in life. Jesus knew the value of spending time with others in more informal settings, and the opportunities that opened up. When he was criticised by the Pharisees for eating with tax collectors and sinners, he said to them: 'It is not the healthy who need a doctor, but the sick. I have not come to call the righteous, but sinners' (Mark 2:17). The healing work of the Lord flows in and through relationships with people around us.

Simple acts of kindness can have a big impact on others, and a far greater effect than we might think. When such acts are a consistent part of how we relate, it will have a positive impact, and particularly if we show kindness to those who are unkind towards us. During the course of the day, and in the midst of our busyness, there will be many opportunities to show kindness through our actions; and a kind act to someone will get noticed. It will be appreciated, even if their initial reaction does not seem to be positive. It can be a way in to build a relationship that could change their life.

Positive and encouraging words can also go a long way. A simple 'thank you' for any help or for work well done can start to sow positive things into lives and can change the working atmosphere. Our words have the power to build or destroy. When James wrote to help Christians with various practical aspects of living out the Christian faith on a daily basis, he noted that whilst the tongue is a small part of the body, it can have an enormous impact (see James 3:1–12.) If the tongue speaks evil, it sets the whole course of a person's life to an eternal hell. It is a bit like the rudder of a ship, which is small but sets the course of the whole ship to its destination. On the other hand, our words can also bring life, healing and goodness to others:

> Reckless words pierce like a sword,
> but the tongue of the wise brings healing.
>
> *Proverbs 12:18*

Positive people who speak positive and encouraging things to others are in short supply. We need to be such people, wherever the Lord has placed us.

Working closely with non-Christians is where we will be challenged to express the love of Christ to those who do not deserve that love. But we did not deserve it either! It is in the workplace where we will come face to face with people who try to harm us or undermine us. We will rub shoulders with those who choose to dislike us, and who make their feelings about us public. There will be people who want to see us fail, and who work behind our back to damage us whilst being friendly to our face. That's people—or at least some people. Every workplace has them. But as champions for God we are called to be different. Our challenge is to live without bearing grudges; to build bridges back to people, even if we are not to blame for the breakdown in a relationship; to forgive, and to demonstrate our forgiveness, and to live in peace with the troublemakers we encounter. Our challenge is to love our enemies, to pray for them and to desire for their lives to be blessed. Jesus told his disciples to,

> Love your enemies, do good to those who hate you, bless those who curse you, pray for those who mistreat you.
>
> *Luke 6:27–28*

This is a tough calling, but as we do things God's way, we can expect Him to protect us and take care of us in a hostile world:

> When a man's ways are pleasing to the Lord,
> he makes even his enemies live at peace with him.
>
> *Proverbs 16:7*

The word of God encourages us to settle matters with any adversaries: 'Settle matters quickly with your adversary..' (Matthew 5:25). We will need to take a positive and constructive approach to resolving any conflicts or differences with others. We may also need to take the first steps, but sometimes it is difficult to know what to do or what to say. Often, people are unaware of the impact on others of their behaviour and words. Here are some tips for helping resolve relationship difficulties with colleagues:

☐ Prayerfully prepare yourself to talk to the other person, and ask others to support you in prayer.

☐ Choose a time and place to talk to the person, that will be least threatening or inconvenient for them. A private place will help minimise potential embarrassment.

☐ Begin the discussion in a positive way. Express appreciation, and emphasise your positive intentions in making the approach.

☐ Clearly state what it is, specifically, about their behaviour, what they say, or other aspects of your relationship that affects you, and describe what impact this has on you and your ability to work effectively. Emphasise that from your perspective the discussion will be completely confidential, and you will not talk to anyone else about it.

☐ Remember there are always two sides to every story, so be prepared to hear some things about yourself that you may not have expected or that may not be pleasant. Be prepared to accept that you may also have misunderstood the other person, or that you may have done something that has had a damaging effect upon them.

☐ Listen, and when you feel the urge to justify yourself, listen some more.

☐ Be prepared to put the past behind you—whether the relationship difficulty is your fault or not.

☐ Try to identify and agree what you, or your colleague, will do or say, or stop doing or saying, that will help you both to work more effectively together.

☐ End on a positive note and try to show that there is no uneasiness between you when you meet later.

☐ Keep on praying, so that the enemy finds no way back in.

PEOPLE WHO ENCOURAGE FELLOW BELIEVERS

There may be opportunities in our daily life to encourage, help and support other believers in the workplace. The word of God prompts us as Christians to be kind to one another, to encourage each other and to build each other up. (See 1 Thessalonians 5:11.) This can be a great help, as many of us face similar difficulties and struggles in the workplace. The love we show is also a witness, and will attract people to want to know more about the good news we have, and to share in the good life that we experience, in Christ.

> 'A new command I give you: Love one another. As I have loved you, so you must love one another. By this all men will know that you are my disciples, if you love one another.'
>
> *John 13:34–35*

SUMMARY OF KEY POINTS

1. Relationships with the boss or colleagues, can present us with some of the most challenging and difficult aspects of our Christian life in the workplace. However, our relationships should be a positive influence for good in the lives of people around us.

2. The starting point for improving our relationships is our self, and more specifically our heart. How much do we really value and care for the people around us?

3. As Christians, we are called to cultivate positive working relationships with our boss, our colleagues and other Christians at work. It may not come easily to us, and it will require effort and humility. If our working relationships are unhealthy, then the time for healing is now.

4. The area of relationships not only provides a challenge for us, it also provides an opportunity to demonstrate Christ to others and to let our light shine in a dark place.

QUESTIONS FOR REFLECTION/DISCUSSION

1. What do you find are the most difficult aspects of building and maintaining positive working relationships with your colleagues?

2. Think of someone you know who gets on well with other people at work. What attitudes and behaviour do they tend to show which seem to help them build good relationships?

3. Think of someone you know who does not get on well with other people at work. What attitudes and behaviour do they tend to show that seem to lead to difficulties in their working relationships?

4. Think of some examples of where poor communication, or miscommunication, has led to conflict or some difficulty in your working relationships. What specific steps could be taken to avoid such problems in future?

5. Read 1 Peter 2:18 and Titus 2:9. From your experience: What are the common struggles or difficulties people face in their relationship with the boss? What lessons have you learned from any struggles that you or your colleagues have had in working with the boss? Should Christians always submit to the boss?

7. Think of an example of when someone was kind or helpful towards you at work. How did it make you feel, and what impact did it have on your working relationship with that person?

8. Why does it seem to be so difficult to show forgiveness to people who harm us? How can we show forgiveness in practical ways?

9. Read Luke 6:27–28. How can the guidance that Jesus gave to his disciples help in the work situation?

10. List the ways in which anything from this chapter or from your review of the above questions applies to you as a working person in your own circumstances. Then list any **actions** you will take as a result of this study (e.g. further study or reflection, prayer, speaking to someone, requests for help, changing something about yourself.) Be as specific as possible about **when** you will complete the action(s).

8

FULFILLING YOUR POTENTIAL

Some employers spend a lot of money training and developing their staff. They realise that developing people to reach their potential and to be well motivated is one way the company can maximise its chances of a successful future. Of course, some companies take the business of developing their people more seriously than others, and some are better at it than others. As Christians we should participate as much as possible in training and development opportunities, as this will help us to do the best job we can, and it can only be a good thing for us and our own future. But fulfilling your potential is about a great deal more than making the most of the development opportunities available. It is about fulfilling God's plan for your life. Fulfilling your potential is therefore not primarily a 'me' centred thing (how can I get the most for myself; how can I develop my skills, achieve career progression or improve my position?) it is a God-centred issue (what does He want to do in me, through me, with me?)

Most of us do not know what God has in store for us—at least, not the full picture. We may not have a clear sense of what He is doing in our life even in the present. We may even look at our working life, workplace and colleagues, and wonder whether the Lord will ever do anything good in and through us, or even whether He would want to! However, if we are open to God working out His plan through our daily life, if we co-operate with Him in faith and trust, and if we persevere, taking one step after another as He leads us through all kinds of experiences, then He will work out His plan. His plan will be good, really good, and a much better one than we could ever design for ourselves. His plan for each of us will have eternal significance, and will dovetail perfectly with the plans He is working out in the lives of other people, though we will probably not be aware of the full picture while we are in this life. His plan is much bigger than we are, and more glorious than we realise or imagine. And the good thing is that we can be a part of it.

He does have a purpose and plan for your life, including your working life, and His desire is for you to fulfil it. Through your varied experiences, struggles and problems, He is shaping your character and strengthening your faith—to prepare you to live with and enjoy Him for eternity. The experiences He puts us through here will have some eternal value. Lance Lambert points out that what God is teaching us at the kitchen sink, or in the factory, at college, or in school is *eternal*.[1] As you obey and serve Him diligently through your work, He will prepare an eternal reward for you. His plan is also to bless others through you, as you touch people with the love of Christ, and as you demonstrate the truth of God in your working life by who you are, by what you say, and by how you work. Finally, His plan is also to bring glory to Himself, as He builds and extends His kingdom through you in the ungodly workplace in which you may find yourself.

God will write history through us if we want Him to and if we allow Him to. Habakkuk wanted God to do something. The cry of his heart was for Him to show His power—to fulfil His plan.

> 'LORD, I have heard of your fame; I stand in awe of your deeds, O LORD. Renew them in our day, in our time make them known; in wrath remember mercy.'
>
> *Habakkuk 3:2*

We can ask God to work something out so that our lives at work will count for something that has eternal value, and so that there will be something to show for our time here. Beside wanting

---

[1] In *Preparation for the Coming of the Lord*, Christian Tape Ministry, Richmond, Va.

God to do something, we must also yield to His work in us. Daniel and Joseph were both working people who allowed God to work out His plan through their working lives. They co-operated with Him every step of the way, even though the steps did not always seem to go onwards and upwards. As a result, God used Daniel to have an impact on the spiritual life of Babylon and beyond, and Joseph was instrumental in saving many lives from death through starvation.

We cannot afford to miss God's plan for our life. When looking back over his successful career, Don Latham noted that: 'In the end all that matters is fulfilling God's purpose for your life.' We must want it and yield to it, because God's plan will be the best that God has for us, and it will take us to a place in life where we are the best we can ever be—where we have fulfilled our potential.

GOD *DOES* HAVE A MASTER PLAN

Our daily life at work will involve success and progress, but we are also likely to face times of struggle, problems and difficulties. There will be times when it is very hard to see any sign of a glorious plan for our life being worked out by the hand of the Lord. If you lose your job, for example, you can find yourself wondering how this can possibly be part of God's plan. We can struggle with the thought that, 'surely His plan is to prosper me and protect me from disaster' —when your experience does not quite seem to square with what you expect. We can feel trapped in a dead-end job, or frustrated if we feel that our progress is being blocked by others. We can see others win favour and get promoted, while we seem to be overlooked, and we can be frustrated when there seems to be no change in the culture of the organisation around us, or in the character and the lives of the people we work with. There are so many ways in which our immediate day to day experience can challenge our belief that God is working out a good plan. However, God *is* in control. Robert Mattox has helpfully suggested that working people need to remember that their future is *determined by their response to God, not by the company they work for*. We often need to remind ourselves of that truth.

But God uses the experiences of life to mould our character and strengthen our faith. Part of His plan is to build 'champions' out of us so that we are more effective for Him in this life and to prepare us to work with Him in eternity. Champions need to go through a tough training programme. That will take time, and will be tailored to include the particular experiences and challenges that we, as individuals, need to go through. His desire is to cultivate in us the character of Christ, and it is often through difficult times that we develop godly qualities and maturity as Christians.

> Not only so, but we also rejoice in our sufferings, because we know that suffering produces perseverance; perseverance, character; and character, hope.
>
> *Romans 5:3–4*

So we need to maintain an eternal perspective and a belief that God is working out a bigger plan than we can see as we face our day to day work activities and struggles. Paul encouraged the Corinthians to see their day to day troubles in the context of God's eternal plan for their lives, and to focus upon the eternal:

> Therefore we do not lose heart. Though outwardly we are wasting away, yet inwardly we are being renewed day by day. For our light and momentary troubles are achieving for us an eternal glory that far outweighs them all. So we fix our eyes not on what is seen, but on what is unseen. For what is seen is temporary, but what is unseen is eternal.
>
> *2 Corinthians 4:16–18*

When James wrote about the value of trials in shaping our character and bringing us to maturity, he also gave a picture of what we can expect after the hard work, trials and difficulties are over:

> Blessed is the man who perseveres under trial, because when he has stood the test, he will receive the crown of life that God has promised to those who love him.
>
> *James 1:12*

It is good for us to hold in mind our eternal prize and destiny, as we press on through the career plan that God has for us.

Our challenge is to believe that He does have a master plan for our lives and that He is working things out for good. He knows the plan that He has for us, even if we only see it in part:

> "For I know the plans I have for you," declares the Lord, "plans to prosper you and not to harm you, plans to give you hope and a future."
>
> *Jeremiah 29:11*

PERSEVERANCE

We will not fulfil God's plan for our life, including our working life, without some effort to persevere on our part, and without help from the Him to see us through to the finish line. Our working life will include difficulties and trials as well as good times. Studs Terkel, in his book *Working*, wrote of work in terms of 'violence to the spirit' and 'daily humiliations' in which, for many people, merely surviving the day is an achievement.[1] If we choose to work to a standard of excellence, and to be positive people who try to change things for the better, then we may find ourselves being the target of resentment and negative criticism from others. If colleagues in the workplace know we are Christians, we will be closely watched, and people will try to test us to see if we are genuine, even seeking to discredit us. If we try to improve the way things are done at work, we may well experience resistance and hostility; the temptation will be to say, 'what's the point?' and to give up. If we try to reach out to people in an effort to build good working relations, we may experience rejection, and it may take sustained effort to break through. If our desire is to see souls saved at work, the devil will try to prevent us from being effective witnesses, and his tactics to disarm or discredit us are always dirty. If we seek to work to God's standard then we can find ourselves being the victims of injustice; wicked people may even seem to be more successful than we are, at least in the short term. When we make mistakes, we will need the courage and determination to pick ourselves up again, learn

---

[1] See S. Terkel, *Working*, 1972, Pantheon Books NY

from the experience, and press on afresh. Ed Cole reminds that champions are not the people who never fail; rather, they are the ones who do not give up.

To be a champion for God in the workplace and to see God's specific plan fulfilled in our working life will therefore require a large measure of perseverance to press on through the difficulties and trials that we face. If we choose to do His will, and fulfil all that He has prepared for us to do, and do it His way, then we will need to accompany that choice with determination, obedience, faith and dependence upon Him to see it through.

Jesus provides a model of perseverance for us to follow. In his earthly life he had an overall goal—to fulfil the will of the Father. He kept this goal in his heart and mind, and even though achieving the goal was a profoundly difficult task, Jesus was determined to see it through. He faced and overcame temptation from the devil. When Jesus was in the desert for forty days, he stood firm and rejected the devil's lies and temptations, using the word of God as his weapon:

> 'Away from me, Satan! For it is written: "Worship the Lord your God, and serve him only."'
>
> *Matthew 4:10*

The Bible teaches us that he was tempted in every way, just as we are. However, he persevered in his obedient and sinless walk with the Father. His was a lonely walk. When he was arrested, in the build up to his crucifixion, we know that his disciples disowned, betrayed, and abandoned him. Peter had said that he would never abandon Jesus, but shortly afterwards that was exactly what he did. When Jesus was about to die on the cross, the profound loneliness and pain of his struggle rang out in his cry:

> About the ninth hour Jesus cried out in a loud voice, "Eloi, Eloi, lama sabachthani?" —which means, "My God, my God, why have you forsaken me?"
>
> *Matthew 27:46*

People conspired and plotted to kill Jesus throughout his ministry. After he was arrested, the Sanhedrin sought to put him to death using false evidence and any means they could. When the soldiers got hold of him, they stripped him, mocked him, beat him severely, and finally nailed him to the cross to die. There was pain and humiliation involved in fulfilling the Father's plan for his life. Despite the injustice, pain, loneliness, and immense struggle he faced, Jesus always adhered to the goal for his life, which was to fulfil the will of the Father. We know there were times when he struggled with this. In Gethsemane when he was overcome with profound sorrow just prior to his arrest, he prayed, "My Father, if it is possible, may this cup be taken from me." However, in the same prayer, he came back to his overriding goal: "Yet not as I will, but as you will." (Matthew 26:39). Only by pressing ahead to fulfil the will of the Father, despite every struggle and difficulty, could he say with his last breath: "It is finished" (John 19:30). He was able to persevere, and overcome the challenges that he faced, through obedient submission to the will of his Father. He chose the Father's way, and His will. He maintained his relationship with the Father throughout his life and ministry. He also exercised his choice and determination to make it through to the end, and to achieve the goal set out for him, and the Father gave him the grace, the strength and the power of the Holy Spirit, to fulfil His plan. Paul taught the church at Thessalonica to model their lives on Christ's perseverance:

> May the Lord direct your hearts into God's love and Christ's perseverance.
>
> *2 Thessalonians 3:5*

To persevere is to be Christ-like. Of course, working life is not all struggle, sorrow and hard slog. It can be enjoyable, rewarding and, at times, fun. We can experience good times and times of blessing. We can get the sense that God is moving us on in His plan. But there are also times when we wish He would move more quickly. I once worked in a company where I became discouraged, and there seemed to be no way out of the circumstances that I was in. I had to wait for God to work something out for me, then to wait a bit longer until I was almost completely at rock bottom. Yet, all the while, God was preparing the next career move for me. It came just in time, and has proved to be a real blessing financially, and in terms of my own development. Sometimes, God wants us to know that He is the one who works things out for good, and not us. Bill Hybels has reminded us that it is a matter of being willing to take small steps in the right 'God-pleasing' direction.[1] We are to look to God for His grace to get us through, and trust that He will perfect by His grace what He has begun in us.

RESIST AND CONFRONT THE DEVIL AND HIS AGENTS

If we set our hearts on fulfilling God's plan for our working lives, the enemy, Satan, will try to prevent us. If the workplace is a place where we want God to be glorified, the devil will try to defeat, disarm, and discourage us there. The efforts of people to distract us, pull us down, discourage us, de-rail or compromise our walk with God, or to destroy us, can all reflect the strategy of the devil to prevent us from fulfilling God's plan in our life. There will be times when we have to make a stand against the work of the devil. We will need to confront the powers of darkness we encounter in the workplace, and enforce God's victory. We must also remember that whilst the enemy can work through people to hinder our progress, our fight is not against people, but against the spiritual forces of darkness at work behind the harmful and wicked things that people do:

> For our struggle is not against flesh and blood, but against the rulers, against the authorities, against the powers of this dark world and against the spiritual forces of evil in the heavenly realms.
>
> *Ephesians 6:12*

So what tactics does the devil use against us? We need to be wise and alert in the workplace, 'in order that Satan might not outwit us' (2 Corinthians 2:11). Here is a brief overview of some of the methods he uses:

Temptation
For Christians in the workplace, there will be temptation to compromise our standards, to sin, or to seek the attractive things

---

[1] See *Faith in the Real World*, Hodder & Stoughton, 1996

of the world above God, such as power, pride which may accompany success, position, prestige and wealth. Ambition can be a good thing, but not if it is all-consuming. Power and authority are good as long as they are used responsibly, but with power comes the temptation to control, dominate and manipulate others for our own ends. There will be many in the workplace who are like the one to whom the psalmist refers who, '...grew strong by destroying others' (Psalm 52:7), and there will be temptation to do the same, particularly if our colleagues are competitive and malicious, and if the culture of the organisation encourages competitiveness and conflict. When people harm us, the temptation will be to harm them back, even by saying something truthful about them but which puts them in a bad light or undermines their reputation. The temptation to be dishonest is common in most workplaces. This can come in various small ways, such as being asked by the boss to say that he or she is in a meeting should there be a phone call, when he or she is actually available to take the call. We can be tempted to cheat the company or our customers, particularly if we are likely to gain more by being dishonest than by maintaining our integrity.

Wearing us down

The devil can try to wear us down through many means; attempting to entice us to fight our battles in our own strength, or seeking to disturb our sleep, so that we become less effective. The enemy would like to get us to fight against people rather than the forces of darkness which may lie behind some human motives. We can be very tempted to retaliate, or fight in the flesh, when someone harms us, rather than calling upon God to fight the battle for us. However, if we fight in the flesh and against the flesh, we will certainly get worn out—and quickly! By contrast, it is those who hope in the Lord who will: 'renew their strength. They will soar on wings like eagles; they will run and not grow weary, they will walk and not be faint' (Isaiah 40:31). If we let the pressures of work and the general busyness of life squeeze out our quality time with the Lord, then we can easily find ourselves weakened spiritually as well as physically and mentally. We are then easy pickings for the devil.

Intimidation

One of the tactics the devil used to try to discourage and distract Nehemiah and the Jews from rebuilding the wall around Jerusalem was mockery and ridicule from the people who were opposed to the work they were doing. Tobiah ridiculed the Jews: '"What they are building—if even a fox climbed up on it, he would break down their wall of stones!"' (Nehemiah 4:3). But Nehemiah was strong enough to resist the mockery, intimidation and jibes. He did not take it to heart, but batted it straight back to where it had come from, pressing on with his work with even greater determination to see it through. We can find ourselves mocked, intimidated and ridiculed as we work to high standards, or simply for being Christians. This can discourage us from being salt and light in the workplace and from doing excellent work— but only if we allow it to.

The fear factor

Fear of man can be a snare to us, and can immobilise our efforts to glorify God in our workplace:

> Fear of man will prove to be a snare, but whoever trusts in the Lord is kept safe.
>
> *Proverbs 29:25*

Threats can have a powerful impact, even on God's champions. Elijah demonstrated enormous courage when he challenged the prophets of Baal, to see whose deity would answer by fire and burn up the sacrifice. God demonstrated His power by burning the sacrifice, and Elijah ordered the prophets of Baal to be killed. However, soon after this great victory over the enemy, Elijah was overcome with fear and ran for his life. This was all because Jezebel threatened that she would kill him in retaliation for what he had done to those prophets: '"May the gods deal with me, be it ever so severely, if by this time tomorrow I do not make your life like that of one of them." Elijah was afraid and ran for his life' (1 Kings 19:2–3). Some managers and colleagues will try to use fear as a tool or weapon, to ensure our compliance and to maintain their power, domination and control over us. We therefore need to be alert to what others are trying to sow into our lives.

People can be bound by fear for many reasons: fear that they could lose their job; fear that if they make a mistake they will suffer; fear that unless they are liked, they will fail; fear that unless they give in to dishonest practices, they will lose their job, or lose favour with people in power. The devil loves to generate fear, as fear is like an invisible prison. It traps us, and will hold us back from moving on in the plan of God with liberty and boldness. Do you feel intimidated by any of your colleagues at work? What effect does that intimidation have on you? We must be set free from fear, and walk in the freedom that Christ has given us if we are to fulfil God's plan for our life, for:

> We have escaped like a bird out of the fowler's snare;
> the snare has been broken, and we have escaped.
>
> *Psalm 124:7*

Direct plots to trap us, destroy us, or ruin our reputation
A young prophet was sent by God to Bethel, to prophesy against the idol worship that had become commonplace under King Jeroboam (see 1 Kings Chapter 13). He went to Bethel and prophesied that the altar for idol worship would be split in half, and in front of the king and the people the prophecy was fulfilled. God had told the prophet not to eat bread or drink water or return the same way that he had gone to Bethel. When the king asked the prophet to stay and eat with him, he was mindful of God's instructions and he refused. However, later, when an old prophet lied to the younger prophet, and told him that an angel had asked him to bring the younger prophet back to his house to eat bread and drink water, the man of God believed him and did as he asked. He was tricked by someone who seemed trustworthy, helpful and credible. He paid for his mistake with his life and he never fulfilled his potential.

In the workplace we need to be wise and discerning, to understand what is going on around us and to be sensitive to the real motives that drive people; we should be aware of the agendas they pursue, behind whatever façade they present. Just because someone is friendly, it does not mean that they are on our side. In my experience, some of the people I have worked with who have seemed helpful and concerned have actually been hatching something against me.

As we have observed, friendliness can open us up, and when we are open we can give away the information they need in order to progress their plans. I am not suggesting that we should cut ourselves off from other people at work, nor that everyone we meet is plotting our downfall. Rather, we need the Holy Spirit to be our close companion, to give us the discernment we need so that we can avoid the traps that the enemy sets for us through other people.

Lies, lies, lies

At work, things we have said or done can be twisted or misrepresented in a way that puts us in a bad light, damages us or spoils our reputation. People can also lie about us. The devil is a liar and leads people to lie. As Jesus said of the devil: 'When he lies, he speaks his native language, for he is a liar and the father of lies' (John 8:44). Joseph worked so conscientiously and effectively in Potiphar's house that his master put him in charge of his whole household. When Potiphar was away, his wife tried to get Joseph to sleep with her. Joseph did the right thing and fled from her. However, when Potiphar returned, she claimed that Joseph had tried to seduce her. Potiphar believed this lie and put Joseph in prison for a crime he had not committed. Joseph was the victim of a malicious lie.

Deception

The devil is the deceiver and he loves to lead Christians astray. When Paul wrote to the Corinthians, he was concerned that the devil might use his cunning to deceive them and lead them astray from a godly life.

> But I am afraid that just as Eve was deceived by the serpent's cunning, your minds may somehow be led astray from your sincere and pure devotion to Christ.
>
> *2 Corinthians 11:3*

Deception can take many forms in the workplace. We may think that a little bit of dishonesty is acceptable, particularly when everybody else cheats customers, the tax man or the company. Of course, it is also wrong to think that poor work and a poor Christian witness at work is somehow compensated for by our faithful and industrious service in the Church context.

Accusations

When Zechariah had a vision of Joshua standing before the angel of the Lord, Satan was right next to him ready to accuse him. The devil is 'the accuser of our brothers' (Revelation 12:10) and in the workplace we can find accusations coming our way from many sources. Many people try to pass the blame and responsibility for a mistake to somebody else; then the innocent person can find himself or herself being accused by the guilty. Does the devil try to make you doubt your own abilities or integrity?

Divide and rule

The devil will try to cause people to rise up as enemies against God's champions. He did so against Joseph, Daniel and Nehemiah, and right in the very place where they were trying to do a good job. People may try to oppose or undermine us and seem to take a dislike to us, for no obvious reason. They can be instruments through whom the devil and his agents try to do his work of spoiling, discouraging and destroying. It was the devil who prompted Judas to betray Jesus: 'The evening meal was being served, and the devil had already prompted Judas Iscariot, son of Simon, to betray Jesus' (John 13:2). There are often different 'factions' in workplaces, and it is all too easy to get drawn into one group that has a grievance or bad relationship with others or even with the boss. The devil likes misunderstandings, divisions, conflict and hatred. Such conflicts will completely undermine our Christian witness, and our goal should be to try to live in peace with everyone whom we work with, even those who seem to be against us.

Direct demonic attack

Direct attack from the enemy can take a variety of forms, such as illness, accidents, fatigue, confusion, self doubt, panic attacks, anxiety, or even job loss. For Saul, a demon tormented him and disturbed his mind. For Job, the enemy caused him physical problems and a series of tragedies. For Jesus, the devil tempted and tested him.

So how can we deal effectively with the tactics of the devil? The following are some principles governing how to resist and overcome the powers of darkness. Whilst these are general principles, they also apply to the workplace. We will, however, need to seek from God His wisdom—and discernment as to how best to defeat the enemy in our own particular circumstances. There may be particular strongholds of the enemy over our workplace, influencing the company culture, the atmosphere, values, relationships and ways of working. We will need to ask God to show us how the enemy is at work, and to give us the spiritual sharpness, as well as the strategies, to bring those strongholds down and to resist and overcome the efforts of the enemy to defeat us.

Clean hands and a pure heart

Maintaining personal holiness in an unholy workplace is a real challenge. Keeping ourselves free from sins such as malice, unforgiveness, anger, lust, selfish ambition and pride in the workplace, where such things may be commonplace, will not be easy. Yet our purity is one of the keys to spiritual victory.

God will protect and vindicate those who are pure and upright. David knew the value of God's favour towards the righteous in the face of enemy attack, and the key role of righteousness in attracting His favour and protection:

> I know that you are pleased with me,
> for my enemy does not triumph over me.
> In my integrity you uphold me
> and set me in your presence forever.
>
> *Psalm 41:11–12*

On the other hand, sin will lead to defeat in any spiritual battle. When we look at the pattern of biblical history, the Israelites experienced defeat at the hands of their enemies when they turned away from God to worship foreign gods, and sinned. When they lost the favour of God through their decision to turn from Him, they discovered that they were powerless to fight back when the enemy came in hard against them:

> In his anger against Israel the Lord handed them over to raiders who plundered them. He sold them to their enemies all around, whom they were no longer able to resist.
>
> *Judges 2:14*

Before we can be effective fighters in the spiritual battle, we need to know where our weak points are, our areas of sin and compromise, our unholy thought patterns and habits, and we will need to deal with them. We must ask the Lord to show us the areas that are to be dealt with, as none of us is good at spotting our weaknesses or seeing our blindspots! This will be painful, and we will need to humble ourselves, repent and change. However, the deeper the purifying and changing work that we allow God to do in us, the greater will be the victory and impact that He can bring through us. If we fail to give over to God all areas of our heart and mind, then those parts which we keep hidden in darkness are the ones in which we may be in danger of being defeated.

To maintain our personal holiness, we will need to be vigilant:

> Be self-controlled and alert. Your enemy the devil prowls around like a roaring lion looking for someone to devour.
>
> *1 Peter 5:8*

When we are tempted to take revenge for an attack or insult, we will need to be self-controlled. We will need self-control when we are tempted to join in the conversation where the boss is being slandered, when we are suddenly tempted to curse someone who has cursed us, and when we feel the urge to be angry and speak obscenities out of frustration or the desire to gain credibility with others. If we fail to be alert, and if we fail to exercise our self-control to resist temptation when it comes, we will be weak against the devil's schemes to prevent us from fulfilling God's purpose and plan. However, if we have clean hearts and are walking right with God, we can be strong against the enemy. Paul Yonggi Cho describes the devil as being like a fly—hating clean places. We need to remove from our lives and minds whatever is not godly, and call upon God to help us avoid falling into sin. The psalmist knew where his weaknesses were, but he also knew where to find strength to overcome those weaknesses:

> Set a guard over my mouth, O Lord;
> keep watch over the door of my lips.
> Let not my heart be drawn to what is evil,
> to take part in wicked deeds with men who are evildoers.
>
> *Psalm 141:3–4*

Walk closely with God

We need God's help if we want to fulfil His plan for our life. We cannot make it on our own, but we have a friend in the highest place to whom we can turn. When we experience success at work, or when things are going well, it can be tempting to think that we can make it in our own strength and through our own abilities. But if we are going to overcome the efforts of the enemy to prevent us from fulfilling God's plan for our life, we must live a life of dependence upon the Lord. King David knew who to turn to when he experienced the attack of his enemies, who were trying to topple him from his position and tear him away from God's plan for his life:

> My soul finds rest in God alone;
> my salvation comes from him.
> He alone is my rock and my salvation;
> he is my fortress, I will never be shaken.
>
> *Psalm 62:1–2*

Our relationship with the Father through Jesus is the source of our strength, protection and power. If we are too busy to spend quality time with God, and if we allow the pressures of life to squeeze Him out of our day, then we lose the source of all our strength and victory. Just as Samson lost his strength to fight and overcome the enemy when he lost his hair, we will also lose our strength to overcome if we neglect our relationship with God. We need to consistently spend time worshipping Him, praying to Him, listening to Him, reading His word; committing all our work plans, daily activities and struggles to Him, and giving Him the glory for the victories and successes, however small. Not only do we need to bring our working life into our relationship with God, we need to bring our relationship with God into our working life. He is the God of our meetings, priorities, presentations, plans, our customer relationships, our computer work, our interaction with colleagues, and all aspects of our working day. We can commit all these things to Him in prayer. We can also call upon Him to help us in moments throughout the day, and ask Him to guide and strengthen us in all we do. If we draw near to God, He will draw near to us—and when He is with us, who can come against us and win?

Speak the truth against lies and accusations

The things that we say can easily get twisted or taken out of context—so much so that a meaning can be placed on what we have said which we never intended. Sometimes, this can be due to genuine misunderstanding, but sometimes people will put their own 'spin' on what we have said in order to support their case against us, or to suit their own agenda—which, as we have observed, may be to harm us. There may also be occasions when lies and accusations are spoken about us, and when we are reported as having said or done things that we have not. There is one simple solution: the truth. We can destroy the power of a lie or accusation by speaking the truth back, not in an aggressive or hostile way, nor in a way that shows we are upset, but rather in a calm, careful, firm and clear way that is sensitive to the culture of the workplace. It is also important to deal with lies quickly before they spread or bed down in peoples' minds as being the truth. We need to be alert and courageous enough to speak the truth against lies as we hear them, and not to walk away feeling hurt, frustrated and angry. Truth is a weapon to defeat our lying enemy, and we need to use it.

Remember Nehemiah completing his great project to rebuild the walls of Jerusalem: enemies tried to prevent him from succeeding, by discouraging and intimidating him. Sanballat and Geshem tried to arrange to meet him, but their intention was to distract him from the work and to find an opportunity to harm him. They sent several messages to try to lure him away, and the fifth message threatened to slander him. This was part of their attempt to force him to meet them. They wrote:

> It is reported among the nations—and Geshem says it is true— that you and the Jews are plotting to revolt, and therefore you are building the wall. Moreover, according to these reports you are about to become their king and have even appointed prophets to make this proclamation about you in Jerusalem: "there is a king in Judah!" Now this report will get back to the king; so come let us confer together.
>
> *Nehemiah 6:5–7*

Nehemiah, champion that he was, destroyed the power of the lie by firing back the truth:

115

I sent him this reply: "Nothing like what you are saying is happening; you are just making it up out of your head."

Nehemiah 6:8

Done!

Pray

Whatever tactics the devil might use to defeat God's champions in the workplace, prayer is a key weapon. As we know, our fight is not against flesh and blood, it is against spiritual forces of darkness, so the weapon we need to fight with must be a spiritual weapon. Prayer, seasoned with the word of God, and directed by the Holy Spirit, is a potent weapon. It is available for us to use to defend ourselves against spiritual attack, or to call for God's help in times of trouble. It is also there for us to use as a strategic and offensive tool, to pray for God's kingdom, pull down the strongholds of the enemy, and to ask God to reveal His will and plan in our workplace. Prayer should be in every worker's toolbox. It should not be left in our churches or homes. We need to use it throughout our working day. Daniel was a working man who found time to pray during his day—it was a priority in his life. He prayed to God prayers of thanks, and he sought Him for help. We need to do the same if we are to see God's plan fulfilled in our own lives, and in the lives of the people around us.

God hears and answers prayer. The psalmist referred to Him in this way: 'O you who hear prayer...' (Psalm 65:2). We can seek God for His help and protection in times of trouble or spiritual attack. The Bible encourages us to turn to God in prayer when we face difficult times:

Is any one of you in trouble? He should pray.

James 5:13

When we pray, God will help us —simple, and true, but how often do we remember to pray when we need help at work? How often do we get bogged down in our struggles or problems without turning to Him in prayer? When the king of Assyria threatened Jerusalem, Hezekiah prayed for God to deliver the people from the enemy. God answered his prayer, and the angel of the Lord killed 185,000 Assyrian soldiers as they slept. Big problem solved! Not all our problems may be solved as quickly, but if we believe in faith that God will help us, and if we depend upon Him, then He will hear our prayers and answer. We may, however, need to persevere in prayer to gain the victory we want.

Prayer is not just a lifeline to God for help in times of trouble, it is also an offensive weapon to fight the enemy. When Paul encouraged the Ephesians to be strong and to take their stand against the enemy, wearing the full armour of God, he highlighted various aspects of the defensive armour—such as the breastplate of righteousness and the shield of faith. He also encouraged them to see that they had at their disposal powerful weapons to be used on the offensive. Another offensive weapon is the sword of the Spirit, which is the word of God:

> Pray in the Spirit on all occasions with all kinds of prayers and requests.
>
> *Ephesians 6:18*

The word of God and prayer make a potent combination— the sword as well as the muscle to wield it. The word of God is like a sharp, double-edged sword in our hand against the enemy, and it can be deployed in prayer. Our prayer life needs to be focused, faithful, fervent and forceful if it is going to be potent for defence and attack. Sometimes it may include fasting.

How wonderful it is that we are able to pray in the Spirit on all occasions. We can pray as we are about to give a presentation to a potentially difficult group of people, as we are about to serve a customer, before writing a letter, answering the phone or doing a calculation. We can pray as we face criticism or conflict, as we are trying to answer a tough question designed to undermine us or when we hear rumours being spread about ourselves, or accusations coming our way. In fact, we can apply the authority delegated by God to His servants; live in His victory, and pray continually—as we face all the challenges and activities of the day, giving the enemy no opportunity to have the upper hand.

Prayer is also more than just an offensive weapon for defeating the enemy and causing him to retreat. It is a means by which we can ask God to establish His kingdom and reveal His purpose and plan in our everyday lives. Prayer is a key for releasing the good, as well as a weapon against whatever is bad. Jesus taught his disciples to pray to the Father:

Your kingdom come, your will be done on earth as it is in heaven.
Matthew 6:10

If we want to see God's purpose and plan fulfilled in and through us, we need to ask Him to do it, and persevere in asking, for prayer is often the condition for fulfilment of divine promises.

Whilst there are many passages from the word of God which can be applied to the huge variety of situations that we may face at work, some especially apt ones are set out below.

PRAYER POWER TOOLS
FOR THE WORKING PERSON

HOPE, ENCOURAGEMENT AND STRENGTH

Commit to the LORD whatever you do,
and your plans will succeed.

Proverbs 16:3

Be still, and know that I am God

Psalm 46:10

Let the weakling say, "I am strong!"

Joel 3:10

The LORD is a refuge for the oppressed,
a stronghold in times of trouble.
Those who know your name will trust in you,
for you, Lord, have never forsaken those who seek you.

Psalm 9:9–10

Why are you downcast, O my soul?
Why so disturbed within me?
Put your hope in God,
for I will yet praise him,
my Saviour and my God.

Psalm 42:11

And we know that in all things God works for the good of those
who love him, who have been called according to his purpose.

Romans 8:28

He gives strength to the weary and increases the power of the weak.

Isaiah 40:29

CHAMPIONS FOR GOD AT WORK

For God did not give us a spirit of timidity, but a spirit of power, of love and of self-discipline.

2 Timothy 1:7

But I am like an olive tree flourishing in the house of God;
I trust in God's unfailing love for ever and ever.

Psalm 52:8

You have not handed me over to the enemy
but have set my feet in a spacious place.

Psalm 31:8

The LORD gives strength to his people;
the LORD blesses his people with peace.

Psalm 29:11

Consider it pure joy, my brothers, whenever you face trials of many kinds, because you know that the testing of your faith develops perseverance. Perseverance must finish its work so that you may be mature and complete, not lacking anything.

James 1:2–4

Blessed are all who fear the LORD,
who walk in his ways.
You will eat the fruit of your labor;
blessings and prosperity will be yours.

Psalm 128:1–2

Lazy hands make a man poor, but diligent hands bring wealth.

Proverbs 10:4

Diligent hands will rule, but laziness ends in slave labor.

Proverbs 12:24

Mightier than the thunder of the great waters,
mightier than the breakers of the sea—
the LORD on high is mighty.

Psalm 93:4

TEMPTATION

Set a guard over my mouth, O LORD;
keep watch over the door of my lips.
Let not my heart be drawn to what is evil,
to take part in wicked deeds with men who are evildoers;
let me not eat of their delicacies.

Psalm 141:3–4

'Get behind me, Satan!'

Matthew 16:23

...we take captive every thought to make it obedient to Christ.

2 Corinthians 10:5

PROTECTION

If you make the Most High your dwelling
—even the LORD, who is my refuge
—then no harm will befall you,
no disaster will come near your tent.
For he will command his angels concerning you
to guard you in all your ways;
they will lift you up in their hands,
so that you will not strike your foot against a stone.

Psalm 91:9–12

Keep me safe, O God, for in you I take refuge.

Psalm 16:1

AUTHORITY, AND VICTORY OVER THE DEVIL

You, dear children, are from God and have overcome them, because
the one who is in you is greater than the one who is in the world.

1 John 4:4

Submit yourselves, then, to God. Resist the devil, and he will flee from you.

James 4:7

The God of peace will soon crush Satan under your feet.

Romans 16:20

Every morning I will put to silence all the wicked in the land;
I will cut off every evildoer from the city of the LORD.

Psalm 101:8

I have given you authority to trample on snakes and scorpions and to overcome all the power of the enemy; nothing will harm you.

Luke 10:19

...If God is for us, who can be against us?

Romans 8:31

May God arise, may his enemies be scattered;
may his foes flee before him.

Psalm 68:1

'I will give you the keys of the kingdom of heaven; whatever you bind on earth will be bound in heaven, and whatever you loose on earth will be loosed in heaven.'

Matthew 16:19

The weapons we fight with are not the weapons of the world. On the contrary, they have divine power to demolish strongholds.

2 Corinthians 10:4

VICTORY OVER OUR ENEMIES

You prepare a table before me in the presence of my enemies.
You anoint my head with oil; my cup overflows.
Surely goodness and love will follow me all the days of my life,
and I will dwell in the house of the LORD forever.

Psalm 23:5–6

FULFILLING YOUR POTENTIAL

When evil men advance against me to devour my flesh
when my enemies and my foes attack me,
they will stumble and fall.

Psalm 27:2

Save me, O LORD, from lying lips and from deceitful tongues.
Psalm 120:2

Do not fret because of evil men
or be envious of those who do wrong;
for like the grass they will soon wither,
like green plants they will soon die away.

Psalm 37:1–2

Contend, O LORD, with those who contend with me;
fight against those who fight against me.

Psalm 35:1

SUMMARY OF KEY POINTS

1. God has a purpose and plan for your life, including your working life. In fulfilling His purpose and plan for our lives, we need to persevere in our faithful service, and depend upon Him every step of the way.

2. We will also need to be wise and alert to the work of the enemy, as he will oppose our efforts to glorify God in the workplace and our desire to see His will done in and through our working lives. If we make our workplace a mission field, then we can also expect it to be a war zone. We need to take our stand against the enemy, and enforce God's victory every day.

QUESTIONS FOR REFLECTION/DISCUSSION

1. Read Jeremiah 29:11. Looking back over your working life so far, can you identify examples of where God has been at work directing the course of events?

2. Describe a time of struggle or difficulty you have experienced in your working life. In what ways did the Lord work things out for good?

3. Describe a time in your working life when it was difficult to see that God was in control. How did things work out?

4. Read James 5:10–11. Consider how these verses apply to you in the workplace.

5. Is it possible for us to step outside God's plan for our lives? How can we avoid doing that?

6. What tactics do you think the devil has used to distract, discourage or tempt you away from following or fulfilling God's purpose and plan in your working life?

7. In terms of fulfilling your potential in your working life, in what ways can God help you? How can you co-operate with Him in this process?

8. Our struggle is not against people, but against the spiritual forces of darkness influencing and working through them. List some of the ways that the forces of darkness are working in your workplace and through other people.

9. Describe a time when you have had to persevere to see a change or breakthrough at work. What helped you persevere?

10. List the ways in which anything from this chapter, or from your review of the above questions, applies to you as a working person in your own circumstances. Then list any **actions** you will take as a result of this study (e.g. further study or reflection, prayer, speaking to someone, requests for help, changing something about yourself) and be as specific as possible about **when** you will complete the action(s).

9

DARE TO BE A DANIEL

When the tiny nation of Judah fell to the might of the Babylonian king Nebuchadnezzar, Daniel was among the Jews who were taken captive and transported to Babylon, the centre of the most powerful empire of its day. Daniel was a very capable young man, with considerable natural ability. He was one of the few young Jewish men specially selected and trained to enter the king's service. During his career he was promoted to high positions in government, becoming a respected administrator and serving under successive kings. While he had great natural abilities and found himself at the top of his profession, it was God who worked through him to demonstrate His sovereign power to a heathen people, and change the spiritual climate of a nation.

God was at work through a courageous believer who lived out his faith with a steadfast determination and simplicity. It was God at work through a man who had a disciplined and consistent prayer life, who lived a life of no compromise, and worked with excellence as his daily standard. This man was a living testimony; God worked out His purpose and plan in him. Daniel's success, and the impact he had as a working person, are an inspirational testimony to what God can do through a worker who commits his life to serving the Lord wholeheartedly in the workplace—like you and me.

There is something all of us can grasp from the life of Daniel, something we can apply in our daily working lives. We may not be in such a high profile and powerful position or have such great natural abilities as Daniel, but God can work in and through us to do great and marvellous things, beyond our imagination. Our task is to believe, and live out the life of a champion—to dare to be a Daniel—and God will do the rest.

A LIFE WITH NO COMPROMISE

Daniel worked in an ungodly environment, yet he resolved in his heart to live his life God's way. The Babylonians served and worshipped false gods, and Daniel and his friends were even named after some of them. In Daniel's workplace it was the norm to find magicians, enchanters, sorcerers and astrologers in positions of influence and even advising the king. This was the occult woven into the very fabric of government. Despite being a prisoner from a small foreign nation, Daniel was faced with an amazing opportunity: to enter the king's service with the prospect of power, influence and wealth. Faced with such an opportunity, many people would have been tempted to compromise, to go with the flow, to fit in with the norms and culture of the workplace. To be different is to take a risk: perhaps that a career opportunity could slip away; or that someone else who is more prepared to conform will be favoured. Daniel did not compromise his walk with God. He kept himself separate from the occult practices that surrounded him. Right at the start of his three year training programme, he refused to take the food and wine offered to him daily from the king's table. What an honour to receive it, and what a risk to refuse it! There was a problem with the food— it had been offered to idols, and the animals had not been prepared according to God's law. Daniel dared to be different, but he did it in a way that kept the peace. He was not offensive, arrogant or 'super-spiritual'. He did not irritate or offend people in the way he expressed his faith, but he found a way to keep everyone happy. He politely, wisely and respectfully asked if the officials would allow him and his friends to try a vegetarian diet, and asked them to test how well they looked after ten days. The concern was that the trainees might not look healthy, and that the person responsible would be punished for not taking good care of them. After ten days, Daniel and his friends looked healthier than the others, so the trial diet was a success all round.

There was pressure to compromise, and not compromising placed Daniel at a disadvantage—even bringing him into danger. The rulers under king Darius were jealous of Daniel's success and the favour that the king showed him. They tried to trap Daniel by persuading the king to issue a decree that anyone who prayed to any god or man other than the king should be thrown into the lions' den. Daniel quietly carried on with his regular prayer time, as he placed God's ways ahead of man's:

> Now when Daniel learned that the decree had been published, he went to his upstairs room where the windows opened toward Jerusalem. Three times a day he got down on his knees and prayed, giving thanks to his God, just as he had done before.
>
> *Daniel 6:10*

His enemies trapped him and, as we know, the king had no choice but to throw him into the lions' den. However, the Lord saved him, and his enemies were fed to the lions instead. Daniel's experience shows that if we are faithful to God and honour Him then He will be faithful to us and honour us. The apparent benefits of compromising can seem great in the short-term, and the cost of commitment can seem very high. However, God blessed Daniel for his faithfulness, prospering him greatly.

The culture of the organisation where we work can push and pull us away from God's ways. It may encourage us to be dishonest, ruthless, harsh, foul-mouthed, blasphemous, materialistic or destructive. We may think that if we do not conform or go with the flow, we will lose favour or credibility, or even lose our job. Some compromises may seem small, and we can easily rationalise them away. If everyone cheats the company over travel expenses—if nobody checks up, or people are not punished for it—the practice can seem normal. But however commonplace and accepted some things are, they can still be wrong. Some areas of compromise may seem large, and we think we would never succumb to them. But the enemy can put us under pressure, drawing us step by step closer to a fall. Whatever the apparent scale of the sin, and whatever the apparent seriousness of the compromise, it is not worth losing the favour and blessing of God in our lives. Daniel tactfully found a way around the problem of eating the contaminated food. He did not compromise, but he did not fall out with his employer over it either. We need to ask God for His wisdom and help if we find ourselves in a position where compromise seems the only way. We must also resolve to follow God, because a working life with Him will be a blessed working life. A working life with compromise will be a life mixed with fear, uncertainty, failure and defeat. We would never fulfil our potential in God that way, and we would end up with nothing. Daniel lived his whole working life without negligence and without corruption—and we can, too.

MAN OF PRAYER

Daniel prayed regularly and consistently throughout his life, maintaining a close walk with God. Three times a day he got down on his knees to pray, offering up thanksgiving, prayer and petitions. Even in the midst of his busy day, and despite all the pressure he must have been under, he made time for prayer. It was a priority on his 'things to do' list. Even when the king decreed that there should be no prayer to God, Daniel maintained a consistent prayer life. He rightly put God's ways above men's ways. His relationship with God was something he maintained throughout his day, and it was part of his life that could not be squeezed or pushed out.

His prayer life was powerful, and it demonstrated what a difference believing in God can make. There was no room for mediocrity, or a quiet life. His prayer life put him at the cutting edge of power and influence in his workplace, and God moved through his prayers to touch and transform lives in that heathen nation. When Nebuchadnezzar ordered the execution of the 'wise men' of Babylon, for not knowing the content of his dream or its interpretation, Daniel asked if he could have some time to find an interpretation. It was a risky offer. When he granted him the opportunity, Daniel urged his friends to plead with God for mercy concerning the mystery of the dream. They sought Him for an answer, in a small prayer meeting. They prayed, and God gave Daniel the revelation that night in a dream. When Daniel shared the dream and its interpretation with the king, he and his friends were promoted to high positions. His courage, backed up by a prayerful reliance upon God, was a powerful key that released God's blessing as well as His purpose and plan. Daniel's prayers were proactive; he sought answers to real problems, and the answers, insights and wisdom God gave him meant that he could make a contribution to the king's affairs that no other worker could provide.

A worker who knows God should stand out from the crowd: the real difference from others is the *power* of God. Through prayer, God can give us answers to questions, solutions to problems, and insights that can be of real benefit to our company and the people working there. Because the answers will be from God, they will work—nobody else will have answers and solutions that work so well. When Solomon prayed for wisdom, God gave it to him. When Elijah prophesied that there would be heavy rain in the time of drought, the rain clouds gathered. When the Lord wanted Joshua and the people to take the city of Jericho, He gave them the strategy for success. So, think about your own workplace. What are the problems that you or your senior managers are struggling to solve? What are the questions they are trying to answer? What a difference it could make if we all learned to work with God's inspiration—and not just with human perspiration!

Daniel prayed with a passion for God and a compassion for people. When he understood that the desolation of Jerusalem would last seventy years, he sought God in fasting, sackcloth and ashes, and intercessory prayer. He turned to Him in worshipful and humble prayer, confessing the sins of the people:

> O Lord, the great and awesome God, who keeps his covenant of love with all who love him and obey his commands, we have sinned and done wrong. We have been wicked and have rebelled; we have turned away from your commands and laws.
>
> *Daniel 9:4–5*

He pleaded that God would turn away his anger and wrath from Jerusalem—for the sake of His name and His people. There was a depth of passion and real urgency in his prayers:

"O Lord, listen! O Lord, forgive! O Lord hear and act! For your sake, O my God, do not delay, because your city and the people bear your Name."

Daniel 9:19

Daniel's prayers were heard by God, and were powerful in the spiritual realm. If we were to pray with the same passion and compassion for the people in our workplace, then God would move and establish His kingdom. We would see change that is not possible merely as a result of human effort. We would see more of His glorious purpose and plan.

MAN OF FAITH AND COURAGE

Edwin Cole has pointed out that 'champions' are those, 'in whom courage has become visible'.[1] Faith mixed with courage was certainly visible in Daniel's life. He had the faith and confidence to believe in God, and the courage to demonstrate his faith through action. When the magicians and enchanters had failed to interpret the king's dream, he expressed ultimate confidence that God could provide an interpretation:

"No wise man, enchanter, magician or diviner can explain to the king the mystery he has asked about, but there is a God in heaven who reveals mysteries."

Daniel 2:27–28

When Daniel interpreted the dream, he was promoted, and the king's awareness of God increased. It was a step on the way to the king's salvation. God gave Daniel the ability and opportunity to make His name known. The power of faith, mixed with the catalyst of courage on Daniel's part, opened up a way for God to move in the circumstances, releasing a greater blessing and revelation of His plan. Where the power of God met with faith in action, He brought about a dynamic change.

Similarly, when Daniel was lifted out of the lions' den, we find that, '...no wound was found on him, because he had trusted

---

[1] See E. Cole, *Courage: Building the Character of a Champion*, Honor Books, Tulsa

in his God' (Daniel 6:23). God protected and honoured the man who trusted in Him. In extreme circumstances, when his life was threatened, Daniel exercised faith and trust in God that he would be kept safe, and his faith was proved right. At such times, Daniel found the power to overcome. The way Daniel reacted to adversity reminds us that in extreme hardship there is a huge difference for believers. We can overcome problems and difficulties, as Daniel did, with complete confidence that the Lord will be with us constantly, and bring us through. Like Paul, we know that nothing can separate us from the love of God.

When Daniel was lifted out of the lion's den, God prospered him, his enemies were killed, and a great witness to the sovereignty of God went out to the nations of the Babylonian empire by decree of the king. No one knows how many people were saved as a result of one man's steadfast faith and courage.

Are there opportunities to demonstrate faith and courage where you work: to trust God when the pressure is on or when you or the company are going through uncertainty; to bring about that change or improvement that other people may not like; to tackle the problem or issue everyone has been avoiding?

MAN OF HUMILITY

Daniel walked humbly before the leaders who were placed over him, showing respect for authority at all times. When king Darius was easily tricked into sending Daniel to the lions, Daniel did not lose respect or honour for his boss, the king. When the king called out to Daniel the next morning, Daniel's first words from the lions' den were: 'O king, live forever!' (Daniel 6:21). The boss had messed up big time, but Daniel's heart remained respectful and humble towards him; he still acknowledged his place under the king's authority. His respect was not contingent upon the king's performance as king. What goes through your mind when the boss makes a mistake that upsets or badly affects you in some way? In most workplaces every mistake by the boss gets reported, discussed, analysed and amplified by the employees.

While Daniel used the gifts of the Spirit so powerfully, and had insight and wisdom that even the king did not have access to, he remained humble. God honoured that humility and used him increasingly, over the course of his life. There was no sense of self-righteousness, nor any judgmental attitude in Daniel, even when he prophesied to those over him that God would judge them. When God gave Daniel the interpretation of Nebuchadnezzar's dream which foretold that the king would be severely humbled by living as an animal for a number of years, Daniel was genuinely perplexed and troubled. Even though his boss was proud and arrogant, and deserved to be humbled, Daniel felt for him, and gently and respectfully offered him the way out:

> "Therefore, O king, be pleased to accept my advice: Renounce your sins by doing what is right, and your wickedness by being kind to the oppressed. It may be that then your prosperity will continue."

> *Daniel 4:27*

Daniel knew his position, despite his talents, wisdom, gifting and the favour of God. He knew his boundaries, and he did not overstep the mark. He never undermined the reputation or position of the king, whatever the king was like, and however badly he did his job.

Daniel also walked humbly before God throughout his life. When the Lord revealed to him the interpretation of Nebuchadnezzar's dream, his first reaction was to praise God:

> "Praise be to the name of God for ever and ever; wisdom and power are his."

> *Daniel 2:20*

Daniel had a clear understanding that the wisdom and revelation he had been given was from God. His first thought was of God—not of any power or influence that might be acquired as a result of being the one to give the correct interpretation. He had a fear and reverence toward God, and his humility gave no foothold to pride, even though the Lord exalted him to a high place and used him so powerfully. He knew that all he had was from God, and was for God's glory. In contrast, it always amazes me how dramatically some people can change (for the worse) if they suddenly get some power or influence for the first time.

AN EXCELLENT WORKER

Daniel worked to a standard of excellence at all times; in everything, he did the best he could—with God's help. Serving under Darius, he was made one of the top three administrators in the country, and he reached high positions under several kings. He excelled at his job, and his excellent work won him favour with his boss, the king:

> Now Daniel so distinguished himself among the administrators and the satraps by his exceptional qualities that the king planned to set him over the whole kingdom.
>
> *Daniel 6:3*

But how did he excel? And what can we learn from his example?

There were four main reasons why Daniel excelled. Firstly, his natural abilities gave him the potential to excel. Daniel was selected for the king's service on the basis of his physical health as well as his aptitude for learning and his quickness of mind. He was equipped for high profile government administration. We all have the potential to excel. It might not be in a comparable sphere, nor at the same level of responsibility as Daniel; but we all have some natural abilities which give us the potential to do well at something.

Secondly, the training he received helped to equip him for service. For three years he studied and was trained to acquire the knowledge, understanding and skills he needed to serve the king as an administrator. His natural abilities gave him the potential to be trained for service, but he needed the training as well as the raw ability. To realise our full potential, and to continue making an excellent contribution to our employer, we too need to get the training and development that will help us to deliver good work in a way that the organisation values. If we neglect our own development and do not keep ourselves up to date, whatever our job, we run the risk of falling behind over time, under-performing, and even losing our position or job, as there may be others with better skills, who are more up to date than ourselves.

Thirdly, he made the *effort* to excel in his work. When the satraps were trying to discredit him out of their jealousy because of his success and the favour that he had won with the king, they could not find any charge against him. In his work there was no corruption or negligence at all. He had a clean track record. He chose to work to the highest standard of excellence despite the standard of those around him, and despite the position and power that he held. He worked to honour God, so much so that even his enemies could not find anything wrong with him or the quality of his work.

Finally, Daniel excelled because of the favour, blessing and anointing of God, who enabled him, and his friends, to be successful:

> To these four young men God gave knowledge and understanding of all kinds of literature and learning. And Daniel could understand visions and dreams of all kinds.
>
> *Daniel 1:17*

These were the God-given abilities that helped Daniel excel in his role as an advisor to the king, and as an administrator. His wisdom, insight and gifts were from God, and these helped him to make a valuable contribution to his employer.

A WITNESS IN HIS WORKPLACE

Daniel's witness for God in the workplace was multi-faceted and powerful. It was about who he was and how he worked as well as what he said—and his life testified to the sovereignty of God. When opportunities arose he was not afraid to speak about his God. When he boldly approached Nebuchadnezzar to pass on the interpretation of the dream, he took the opportunity to witness. Daniel told him that there was no point in turning to his magicians and enchanters, but that, 'there is a God in heaven who reveals mysteries' (Daniel 2:28). He pointed the heathen king to the one true, all-powerful God. He even tried to point him to repentance, but he did so sensitively, tactfully and respectfully. Daniel's words were only taken seriously *because* his witness for God was much more than words. It was the quality of his life, and the quality of who he was as a person, that gave the words their credibility. He worked with integrity, honouring his boss. Even his enemies could not fault his standards. Paul Yonggi Cho has rightly observed that it was through the quality of his life that Daniel was an excellent preacher of God. Because of the quality of his work, he was valued and appreciated by each king he served. For example, when he was thrown into the lions' den, Darius was greatly distressed, saying: 'May your God, whom you serve continually, rescue you!' (Daniel 6:16). The king was perplexed all night. He could not eat or sleep at the thought that Daniel was in the lions' den, and his distress only lifted in the morning when he saw that Daniel was safe. Daniel showed his faith, godliness and courage to all. He trusted in God, and people could see that his God vindicated and blessed him, time after time. It was real. Not everyone liked it, and he certainly had enemies who tried to destroy him. However, he remained steadfast and God prospered him in the sight of his enemies and destroyed those who sought to destroy him. God upheld him in his integrity and everyone could see that Daniel's God was alive and real.

Through Daniel's prophetic gift, God was able to demonstrate his sovereign power and righteousness to the heathen. Daniel told Belshazzar the meaning of the message that the mysterious hand had written on the wall, and that God had judged him for his pride and for using the temple goblets as drinking vessels. He told him that his reign was at an end—and that night Belshazzar was killed. There must have been a fear of God after that prophecy came to pass so swiftly and accurately!

Daniel had to persevere in his faithful and consistent witness to those around him, and it was the work of a lifetime. After he interpreted Nebuchadnezzar's dream, the king seemed to grasp something of the reality of God:

> 'Surely your God is the God of gods and the Lord of kings and a revealer of mysteries, for you were able to reveal this mystery.'
> *Daniel 2:47*

However, the next thing we read in the account is that Nebuchadnezzar erected a ninety foot golden idol, and commanded everyone to worship it. Daniel's was a tough mission field. But he pressed on, and eventually God broke into the king's heart, humbled him and changed him. The king went on to issue a testimony to the power of Daniel's God to all peoples, but it was twenty years before Daniel saw that breakthrough. He had sown years of faithful and faultless witness before he saw the king turn to the Lord. Then when Nebuchadnezzar's son took over as king, the spiritual progress must have seemed to have been lost. He was a sinner with no regard for God. But Daniel pressed on, and the next king, Darius, turned to God following the witness of Daniel, and he even issued a decree that everyone should fear and reverence God.

During Daniel's lifetime there were seasons of patient witness to the heathens around him, as well as seasons when the kingdom of God advanced significantly. But whatever the season, Daniel remained consistent, steadfast and strong in his walk with the Lord—witnessing in his workplace to the sovereignty and reality of God.

A MAN THROUGH WHOM GOD WROTE HISTORY

The whole of Daniel's life was a testimony to the sovereign God who is in control; who has charted the course of history, and is working it all out step by step. God brought Daniel to a heathen land—subsequently working in his life, and the affairs of men, to place him in positions of influence and power. Under Nebuchadnezzar he was made ruler over the entire province of Babylon, and under Belshazzar he was made third highest ruler after he was brought back from a time in obscurity. Under Darius he was also given high office. God chose to place a devout follower, a trusted disciple, where He could use him—to demonstrate His own glory and power, and to make His name known to the lost. In fact, God so worked through Daniel that the heathen kings became the evangelists for him. Nebuchadnezzar wrote to the peoples of the world explaining how he came to know God, and how God had worked in his life for good. Darius also wrote to all peoples, nations and men of every language throughout the empire, following the demonstration of God's power in saving Daniel from the lions. What a testimony it was:

'I issue a decree that in every part of my kingdom people must fear and reverence the God of Daniel. For he is the living God and he endures forever; his kingdom will not be destroyed, his dominion will never end. He rescues and he saves; he performs signs and wonders in the heavens and on the earth. He has rescued Daniel from the power of the lions.'

Daniel 6:26–27

When Daniel stood firm in his faith during testing times, God worked out a greater witness to His own power than Daniel could ever have hoped to achieve by his own efforts or abilities.

God found in him a man through whom He could work out His plan and purpose, and worked through events to prosper him, protect him, and reach a lost people. He left an eternal legacy of souls, as well as prophetic revelation that is relevant to the people of God even in these last days. God uses the small and unlikely things to demonstrate His greatness. By walking humbly before God, allowing Him to use you, showing faith and courage like that of Daniel—in whatever employment environment you find yourself—yours can be a powerful witness. God can write history through ordinary people, like you and me.

SUMMARY OF KEY POINTS

1. God can fulfil a specific purpose through your working life. He can place you where He wants you to be, and if you are willing then He will work in you and through you, to fulfil that purpose and create an impact on the world.

2. Daniel had a powerful mix of qualities. He had faith and trust in God, as well as the wisdom, courage and commitment to follow Him. Spiritual gifts were also in operation in his working life. He had a practical and self-disciplined approach to prayer, worship and learning, and an openness to be used by God. These qualities in action provide an effective channel for God to impact any work environment, however heathen.

3. Our destiny is in the hands of God, not in the hands of men. God promotes and prospers us, as He did Daniel. Our task is to honour Him in all that we do.

QUESTIONS FOR REFLECTION/DISCUSSION

1. Read Ephesians 5:15–16. What pressures (subtle or obvious) do you face, to compromise your Christian faith or standards in your workplace?

2. Read Daniel 2:17–19 and 6:10. What aspects of Daniel's prayer life could you usefully apply in your working life?

3. Describe a time when you had to trust that God would protect you, help you or work something out for you. How did things work out?

4. How does pride tend to show itself in the attitudes and behaviour of people at work?

5. Daniel's workplace was strongly influenced by the occult. What evidence of the occult do you see in your workplace or in the lives of people you work with?

6. What are some of the problems or questions that your more senior managers are trying to address? How can you bring God into the situation to help?

7. In what way might you need to 'dare' to be a Daniel where you work?

8. What is it about Daniel's character and approach to working life that you admire or respect most?

9. List the ways in which anything from this chapter, or from your review of the above questions, applies to you as a working person in your own circumstances. Then list any **actions** you will take as a result of this study (e.g. further study or reflection, prayer, speaking to someone, requests for help, changing something about yourself) and be as specific as possible about **when** you will complete the action(s).

10

WHEN LIFE IS STRANGER THAN FICTION

─────────────

Real life can be stranger than fiction, especially when the Lord is in control. Joseph's life, like Daniel's, demonstrates how a life lived for God in the workplace can be stranger (but more glorious) than fiction could ever be.

As a young man, Joseph looked after his father's sheep in Canaan until his brothers sold him into slavery. He was taken to Egypt, where he later became governor, second only to Pharaoh himself, and this was in a land where shepherds were despised. Before his appointment as governor, he served as the manager of the household of Potiphar, captain of the guard. He was wrongfully imprisoned, but even in the prison he was an exemplary worker, looking after the prisoners. Through such an unlikely route, and through such adversity, God was at work, shaping and preparing him, and working out a career path for him to reach high office. When Joseph was in prison, he interpreted a dream for one of the prisoners. The prisoner was released, and when he found that Pharaoh needed someone to interpret a dream, he remembered Joseph. Joseph was then taken from prison. He was given a chance to clean himself up, and was then brought before Pharaoh to interpret his dream. He interpreted the dream successfully, and later was put in position as the highest administrator in Egypt. In this position he initiated and led a God-given famine relief strategy that was to save Egypt and the surrounding nations from starvation. His job also opened the way for a wonderful and emotional family reunion as his brothers were drawn to Egypt for food. God was also working something else out through all this, something of eternal significance. By saving his brothers from starvation, Joseph's work also protected the birth line through Judah to Jesus, ensuring that God's promise to Abraham of many descendants was fulfilled. Only God could have done all this!

Not all of us are destined for such high office, but there is much we can learn from Joseph's life, to help strengthen and build us up as workplace champions. As in the case of Daniel, Joseph's character is a model for us. He was faithful, and he demonstrated the responsible use of power and God-given authority. He showed wisdom and godliness in the way he managed. Like many of us, he worked in a hard and ungodly environment, yet he was like a fruitful vine, a channel through whom God blessed people, and an instrument through whom God fulfilled His plan. His life is an encouragement to us—to live our working life for God.

LIFE IS A LEARNING EXPERIENCE

In these days of rapid technological change, with information technology playing a greater role in our day to day work, and with the development of global markets, companies are placing greater emphasis on the ability of the workforce to learn, adapt and change. Business is looking for people who can learn new skills quickly, do things better, cheaper, more efficiently and to a higher standard.

To be workplace champions we need to be learners. We need to learn from our experiences, including our mistakes, and apply the lessons learned in a way that makes us more effective. We must also be open to God dealing with us, changing and developing us, so that we can move further on in His purpose and plan—even if this means learning our lessons and making our mistakes in lowly positions first, or going through times of adversity, before He leads us on to positions of greater responsibility and influence.

To reach high office, Joseph had to learn from his experiences. He often had to learn the hard way, too. As a young man, Joseph was his father's favourite son, and his brothers hated him because of their jealousy. When he told his brothers of a prophetic dream which foretold that he would rule over them, their hatred towards him was inflamed. Joseph could not keep the dream to himself. At that stage he had no discretion and little wisdom. He was not alive to the interpersonal dynamics of the family. In his excitement and naïvety, he blurted out:

> "Listen to this dream I had: We were binding sheaves of grain out in the field when suddenly my sheaf rose and stood upright, while your sheaves gathered around mine and bowed down to it."
>
> *Genesis 37:6–7*

They were furious, but he went even further and urged them to listen to a second dream, in which, he says, 'the sun and moon and eleven stars were bowing down to me' (Genesis 37:9).

Shortly after this, they sold Joseph into slavery, and some of his brothers also came close to killing him for what he had said. At this stage in his life, Joseph does not sound much like a diplomatic or insightful governor, skilled in dealing with people and matters of national and international significance. Joseph had a lot of learning to do, but his life shows that there is hope for us all! As governor of Egypt we find him a changed man. When his brothers came from Canaan to buy grain from him, they did not recognise him, but Joseph recognised them. They bowed down to him, thereby fulfilling the prophecy he had told them about before they sold him into slavery. During the conversation he had with them, he was so emotional that he had to turn away and weep, but he chose not to reveal his identity to them at that point. He had clearly learned to exercise self-control and restraint of his tongue, even though he was longing to speak out what was on his heart. Similarly, when his brothers came to him the second time, they had Benjamin with them. However, he still did not reveal his identity to them, despite being deeply moved when he saw them, and despite the overpowering urge to show his love to Benjamin.

As governor, we find him to be a man who was able to relate tactfully and effectively to others. When he was preparing his brothers for their introduction to Pharaoh, he anticipated that Pharaoh would ask them about their occupation. Joseph counselled them to tell Pharaoh that they tended livestock rather than mentioning sheep. Here is a man who had learned to understand and anticipate the impact of what was said on the feelings and thoughts of others. He had learned the art of diplomacy. He did not encourage his brothers to lie, just to communicate in a way that was sensitive to the likely reaction of the listener. What a difference from the young man who had inadvertently fuelled their hatred by tactless comments.

We also see that, as governor, Joseph had developed the ability to deal with others as the man in charge. He was no longer the shepherd boy, bullied by his brothers. He had learned how to present himself, how to communicate, and how to think quickly in a way that reinforced his authoritative position and helped him achieve his objective. When his brothers first visited Egypt in search of food, they were without Benjamin, but, when they mentioned him, Joseph was quick to find a way to force them to bring Benjamin to him. Joseph accused them of being spies, but by bringing their youngest brother to him they could prove the truth of their word that they were only in search of food. Joseph was sharp now, quick-witted, and able to work through other people to achieve his own ends. He is firm with them; he has strength of character, and he makes it clear that they are operating on his terms. No longer the naïve shepherd boy who fell into the traps that his brothers set for him, he had become the man in authority:

> On the third day, Joseph said to them, "Do this and you will live,
> for I fear God: If you are honest men, let one of your brothers
> stay here in prison, while the rest of you go and take grain back
> for your starving households. But you must bring your youngest
> brother to me, so that your words may be verified and that you
> may not die."

Genesis 42:18–20

Of course, Joseph would not have killed his brothers, but they were left in no doubt about who was calling the shots. He now had the confidence, firm character and skills needed to lead with authority.

Joseph's training ground had been in humble circumstances, and his abilities and character had developed through times of adversity. He could not enter high office directly from being a shepherd boy, but God put in his way the right stepping stones. God had a tailor-made career development plan for Joseph, just as He has for us. Joseph's first exposure to administrative work was on a small scale—as the manager of Potiphar's household—but this experience was formative. Joseph excelled in his work, with God's help, and Potiphar placed him in charge of everything to do with the running of the household. This was Joseph's first taste of being the man in charge. In this environment he not only learned the administrative skills that he would later need on a larger scale, but he also began to *see himself* as the man in charge, which was necessary preparation for leadership. He needed to become a leader on the inside, before he could demonstrate it on the outside. He had to leave behind the 'shepherd boy' and think of himself in a different way. His emerging self-image as a figure of authority, acquired in Potiphar's house, was still a little brash and rough around the edges, but his self-assurance as a leader was developing. Joseph's emerging sense of authority is evident in his reply to Potiphar's wife when she tried to entice him to have sex with her:

> "With me in charge," he told her, "my master does not concern himself with anything in the house; everything he owns he has entrusted to my care. No one is greater in this house than I am."
>
> *Genesis 39:8–9*

If you are working in humble circumstances, or if you are going through adversity at work, be encouraged. God may be moulding and shaping your character so that He can move you on in His plan for your life. It may take faith to believe it as you look at where you are now, but be reassured by the life of Joseph—all things are possible for God!

The next step in God's learning and development plan for Joseph came during a time of adversity, when he was wrongfully imprisoned. It might have looked like a backward step in terms of his career and life, but God knew what He was doing. The rough edges of Joseph's character still needed smoothing; here was another place where God positioned him and galvanised further Joseph's sense of being the man in charge. The Lord gave him success in prison, and favour with the guard; and he was quickly put in charge of the prisoners and the day to day running of the prison:

> ...The warden put Joseph in charge of all those held in the prison, and he was made responsible for all that was done there. The warden paid no attention to anything under Joseph's care, because the Lord was with Joseph and gave him success in whatever he did.
>
> *Genesis 39:22–23*

In adversity, Joseph proved that he was prepared to work to an excellent standard and to serve wholeheartedly, despite the lack of reward. He proved his integrity as an excellent worker. His integrity and trustworthiness was going to be an important quality later, when he had responsibility, as governor of Egypt. He did not compromise his standard of integrity in small things, and God was then able to trust him with more. Joseph's prison experience also taught him to step quickly into the position of the man in charge. He rapidly took charge of the caring and managing aspects of prison life. This was necessary preparation because when he was later asked to lead the famine relief strategy, he had to step into the role immediately. He was ready to take charge when it was time to take on the bigger task.

In prison he also learned the hard lesson that God was in control of his career, and that he needed to patiently trust Him to work things out—in *His* timing and in *His* way. When Joseph interpreted the dream for the cupbearer and baker, he asked the former to put in a good word for him to Pharaoh when he got out, thereby trying to work out his own escape route. However, the cupbearer forgot about Joseph, and two long years passed before he remembered him—when Pharaoh needed someone to interpret his dream. Then, when Joseph was brought before Pharaoh, he was almost immediately promoted to high office. All the preparation time had paid off. It had been a tough experience, but a formative and necessary one for him, to prepare and change him for greater things. God's succession and development plan was perfect. The best thing we can all do is to submit to God when He works in our life through adversity and trials and in humble circumstances. It will be for good in the long run, even if it feels painful and does not seem to make sense at the time.

A GODLY MAN

The key to Joseph's success did not lie in his abilities, great as they were; it was God who made the difference. Because God was with him throughout his career—from Potiphar's house to governor—his career prospered. Joseph found favour and success beyond what he could have achieved by his own efforts or through his own abilities. He lived his life to a godly standard, and it was God who opened the doors for him and moved him on. Joseph walked closely with God, and God walked closely with him.

Joseph resisted, avoided and even fled from sin. It had no place in his life. Remember when Potiphar's wife persisted in her attempts to get Joseph to have sex with her, he was steadfast in his resistance: 'And though she spoke to Joseph day after day, he refused to go to bed with her or even be with her' (Genesis 39:10).

Here was constant and persistent pressure to give in, matched by firm and consistent resolve not to. Some traps are persistent and constant in intensity, whilst other traps for us to compromise can spring up more suddenly. When Potiphar's wife became more desperate, she tried to force him to meet her demands. She attempted to ensnare him by grabbing his cloak and saying: "come to bed with me!" He fled as quickly as possible. In the workplace, temptations and pressures to compromise come in many forms. Some are a constant temptation in the background, and some happen more suddenly. Unless we are both strong and vigilant, we can stumble. The devil would love to defeat workplace champions, and he sets traps for us. What pressures to compromise do you face in your workplace—corruption, lies, deceit, revenge, or the abuse of power?

As we have seen, Joseph's older brothers wronged him when he was a teenager. Over twenty years later, when Joseph came face to face with his brothers again, he had the power of life and death over them. He had the opportunity to take revenge, but instead he blessed them in a marvellous way. On their first journey he placed grain in their sacks and gave them their money back. When they returned a second time, he honoured them with a feast. He loved his brothers, and when he finally revealed his identity to them, he embraced them and reassured them that he harboured no bitterness in his heart. Instead, he settled his brothers and father, providing the very best for them. He went beyond forgiveness to show them kindness and love. Does forgiveness mark your working relationships? In the workplace, it is easy to feel bitterness and resentment against those who have wronged us. As David found, there may be people who seem to come against you for no obvious reason: 'Many are those who are my vigorous enemies; those who hate me without reason are numerous (Psalm 38:19). God's champions should be 'teflon coated' —sin, bitterness, hatred and unforgiveness do not stick to them!

Complete integrity characterised Joseph in all his workplace dealings. Potiphar entrusted the management of his whole household to Joseph. He did not need to check up on him. The prison guard also let Joseph get on with looking after the prisoners and making sure the prison was running well. He had every opportunity to be dishonest in small things. But he passed the test, and God was later able to trust him to manage the vast wealth generated through the famine relief strategy and the huge responsibility associated with that job. Joseph could have been dishonest and gained great wealth. As Charles Swindoll has noted, Joseph's leadership position would have provided ideal opportunities for corruption—lining his own pockets and those of his friends. He had real power and influence, but was careful not to abuse the trust and power that he had been given. He was a good steward of all that was entrusted to him.

He was careful to give God the credit. When Pharaoh summoned Joseph to interpret his dream, he was careful to ascribe the ability to God, saying, "I cannot do it... but God will give Pharaoh the answer he desires" (Genesis 41:16). This was the door to high office opening for him, and he was careful to give God the glory. It was God who was in charge of Joseph's life, enabling him and guiding him, and Joseph was careful to give Him the credit. There was no credit grabbing when he had the opportunity to be the centre of attention. Even after several years of great success and high office, he was careful to acknowledge that it was God who had given him the high position to fulfil His purpose and plan. When speaking to his brothers, he said: "...it was not you who sent me here, but God. He made me father to Pharaoh, lord of his entire household and ruler of all Egypt" (Genesis 45:8). Joseph never let the power or success that he had go to his head. He knew it was all from God, and all for God's glory.

A MAN OF GOD

Joseph was a man of God who allowed God to work through him, to fulfil His purpose. As with Daniel, it was a particular spiritual gift, the interpretation of prophetic dreams, that opened a door to high office; so that God could use him. When, in prison, Joseph interpreted the dreams, his God-given interpretation came true. Two years later, when Joseph interpreted Pharaoh's dream, Pharaoh could see in Joseph a degree of wisdom and ability that nobody else had, and then he appointed him to lead the famine avoidance strategy. God gave Joseph a gift that made all the difference. It was so useful to his boss, and marked Joseph out from the crowd.

Through spiritual gifts, God's wisdom and power are released to address real practical issues, so it is surprising how little we hear about the use of these gifts in the work context. Yes, the gifts of the Spirit are for the building up of the body of Christ, but the New Testament depicts their use to bring conviction, healing and revelation to sinners in everyday life. If God opens up His plan and purpose through the exercising of spiritual gifts, then perhaps those of us who have never used the gifts in the work context are missing out on something powerful. Perhaps, our workplaces are also missing out on a demonstration of God's power to deal with the big problems and issues of the day. What should our sales strategy be? What should we invest in? Which contractor or supplier should we work with? How can we improve the way we make our product or deliver our service so that we will be successful? Who should we promote? Who should we select? How should we tackle that problem that has been around for a long time? What is really bothering him? The list could go on. Yet, many of us probably shy away from using the gifts of the Spirit even in the church context, so it is not surprising that we are cautious in the workplace too. But, if we are prepared to be open to God using us in this way, and are willing to learn from our experiences—and even our mistakes—then we can have a greater impact for God on our places of work, making a contribution that others never could. This is part of the difference knowing God can make. Pharaoh saw something unique in Joseph—and it was wisdom and discernment from God. Through the demonstration of that wisdom and insight God blessed Joseph. It also opened up a great blessing for the nation and the surrounding nations. Perhaps now is the time to expand our vision for workplace ministry and embrace the gifts of the Spirit. Who knows what God will do through us! I was once with a Christian work colleague and we were having a regular prayer time during our lunch hour. It came to me that the person had difficulties in the relationship with their sister, and that the Lord wanted the relationship to be repaired before they left home to get married. I already knew about the impending marriage, but had no idea that there was a sister, nor that all was not well in their relationship. When I said it, the colleague's jaw dropped with amazement. There was indeed a sister—and a lot of bad feeling between them. Clearly, the Lord had put his finger on an area of that person's life which needed to be dealt with—as, happily, it was.

Consider these brief definitions of some of the gifts of the Spirit, and think about how useful they could be if applied in your workplace:

The gift of faith

Saving faith, by which we receive Jesus and become Christians, is a gift of God; salvation is by grace, through faith. There is also the faith which we must exercise when we pray—Jesus commands us to 'have faith'. We are to believe, rather than be doubters. There is also the gift of faith that rises up in us when we are to minister to someone else in some way, perhaps for healing, or to meet a particular need. We simply 'know' that the moment is God's, and that it is right to go ahead boldly. The Holy Spirit puts in our hearts such faith that God will act in a situation. The test of the reality of such promptings, as always, is in the fruit, and in fidelity to the revealed word of God.

The word of knowledge

The Bible testifies throughout to the truth that God speaks to people. A Christian filled with the Holy Spirit can expect to hear from God, and sometimes such 'words' will have very specific significance, pinpointing something that needs ministry. Often, words are received and applied in prayer ministry, including but not limited to, the ministry of healing. Closely allied to this are 'pictures' which come to us. Again, applying biblical criteria is vital to evaluating 'words' and 'pictures'.

The word of wisdom

This signifies words, or guidance, from the Lord which show us how and when to apply things He has shown us. It is not always right to release what we hear. Some words are for us alone; some for others at a later stage; some to show us how to pray for others. We need God's wisdom to know what to do with a word.

Gifts of healing

The Bible shows several models for healing: intercession in the presence, or at a distance from, the sick person; speaking to the sufferer; laying-on-of-hands; speaking to the condition; anointing with oil. Holy Spirit-led ministry of healing always glorifies Jesus, and can take any of these biblical forms.

Miracles

We see many examples of miracles—things which cannot be brought about by natural means—in the New Testament. God's nature does not change; He can work miracles today, and He sometimes uses believers in this way.

Prophecy

Sometimes, a word from the Lord can be for encouragement, edification or challenge. Paul is extremely positive about this spiritual gift: 'I would like every one of you to speak in tongues, but I would rather have you prophesy' (1 Corinthians 14:5). The words received must be 'weighed' by others with this gift.

Gift of discernment

This has to do with being made aware by the Holy Spirit of the spiritual forces at work around us. It is a key to effective prayer ministry.

Tongues

We may pray with understandable words (i.e. in known languages). We can also be enabled by the Holy Spirit to pray, speak or prophesy in a heavenly language or 'tongue'.

Don Latham provides numerous examples of effective use of gifts of the Holy Spirit in workplace ministry. He writes:

> A colleague had had serious surgery and, when we met in the lift one day, it was quite natural for me to ask how he was. He described pains in his body, and a ringing noise in his head, from the time he woke up to the time he went to sleep. I felt compassion and, instantly, a thought came into my mind,
>
> 'Pray for him; I want him to be healed.'
>
> 'You don't pray for people in lifts,' was my next thought. 'He is a subordinate of mine. What if nothing happens?' By the time I had listened to these doubts we had reached the third floor and gone our separate ways. 'I blew that, Father, bring him to my office if you want me to pray for him,' I said, sitting at my desk.
>
> A few moments later there was a knock on my door. I had no doubt who was standing the other side. He came in and, after we had briefly discussed some matters of finance, I said to him, 'I believe God wants me to pray for you, and you are going to be healed.'
>
> Please pray,' he said. I went round my desk, gently laying hands on his shoulders and, not knowing how to pray in English, prayed in tongues. It all seemed natural—not least to my secretary, who sat in the room next door and could see what was happening, because the door was open. She went on typing, as though we did this every day!
>
> A few months later, this colleague told me that, from the day we prayed, the noise, which I was to discover was called tinnitus (and was incurable), had diminished day by day, until it had gone completely. More importantly, through the intervention of another Christian colleague, he had made his own personal commitment.[1]

John Kelly and Paul Costa also see great potential value in Christians using the gifts of the Spirit in the workplace—to make a real difference. While they acknowledge that this can be intimidating for us, their message is a challenging one, that, 'we need to have the courage to use our gifts outside church

---

[1] See D. Latham, *Being Unmistakably Christian at Work*, Terra Nova, 2000

walls.' They give examples of how someone was used in the gift of prophecy to help point to which stock to invest in, and of another who dramatically increased his earnings when he started to use his prophetic gifting to determine where to win business contracts. There are clearly dangers in all this, particularly using the things of God to gain material wealth. Certainly, Joseph and Daniel prospered materially, but they also bore witness to the power and greatness of God in heathen nations, and they were used as a channel of blessing. Using the gifts of the Spirit in the work context, we need spiritual covering, and accountability to the local church. However, it is clear that, as we read about Daniel and Joseph, many of us are not bringing God into the workplace in a way that will make a profound and real difference, and we need to learn more from God in this area of workplace ministry. It is certainly easier to brush it to one side than to take risks and be open to the possibilities that could open up if we were to ask Him to use us.

MAN OF VISION AND ACTION

When he was brought to Pharaoh to interpret his dream, Joseph was told by God that seven years of abundance would be followed by seven years of severe famine. Joseph knew that God had decided this would happen—and soon. In the face of this impending catastrophe, Joseph articulated a way forward, a vision of how to deal with the problem, and a strategy:

> "And now let Pharaoh look for a discerning and wise man and put him in charge of the land of Egypt. Let Pharaoh appoint commissioners over the land to take a fifth of the harvest of Egypt during the seven years of abundance. They should collect all the food of these good years that are coming and store up the grain under the authority of Pharaoh, to be kept in the cities for food. This food should be held in reserve for the country, to be used during the seven years of famine that will come upon Egypt, so that the country may not be ruined by the famine."
>
> *Genesis 41:33–36*

His God-inspired vision was to save Egypt from starvation. Leaders would be appointed to store food during times of plenty, so that there would be enough during times of famine. Collecting a fifth each year, rather than a seventh, also ensured that there would be enough food to sell to the surrounding nations during the famine. It was a simple but effective strategy, and we know that it worked.

Not only did he have a God-given vision, and a strategy that he communicated to others, Joseph was also involved in making sure it delivered the results—through to completion. He travelled throughout Egypt, ensuring that food was collected and stored; and, when famine came, he took charge of the sale of the grain. He saw the strategy through, made it his own and gave his best effort to ensure its success. Through his work, he delivered what was required. There will be little success for the worker who does not keep delivering what the organisation requires, and in a way that the organisation requires it. It may sound obvious, but there are many people who think that their employer owes them a living: giving only the minimum effort—or even less than the minimum. I know a well qualified manager who kept losing his job. He thought that his employer employed him because he was well qualified and clever. But after he was made redundant twice, he finally realised that his employer had paid him to deliver the work that the company wanted done. That was a turning point in his life; after that he started to work well, and has been successful ever since. He has managed to secure a job with good pay, and was highly rated in his performance assessment. Some people also come to work for the social life, rather than to deliver a good day's work in exchange for their pay.

I have known people who have been frustrated at not getting promotion. However, in many cases there is a good reason why they have not been successful, such as laziness or a poor attitude towards the company or senior colleagues. I have found, though, that many such individuals either cannot seem to see why they are not getting on, or refuse to flow in with what the company wants from them.

When he was governor, Joseph's vision of famine relief was on a national, and international, scale. But his vision encompassed small things too, affecting everything he did. When working as a household manager for Potiphar, his aim was to give excellent service, and to be the man in charge of a well managed operation. He worked to fulfil that vision wholeheartedly.

Similarly, in the prison his aim was to provide an excellent and caring service to the prisoners and to manage the operation well on behalf of the guard. His life was about excellence, success and service in everything he did. His vision and values guided his action.

As working people serving God through our work, we too need to be people of vision. Vision is about seeing the possibilities; about aspiring to something better or higher. It is about seeing where you are aiming for before starting the journey. It is about establishing God's way, seeing what He wants to do, or how He wants to change the way things are. What do you think God wants to see or do in your workplace? How do you think He wants to see you and your colleagues working? It could be: providing excellent customer service; more efficient and ethical use of resources; better management of people; growth; strong leadership; highly effective team-work; a more positive and motivating culture; an honest and polite operation. The possibilities are endless, but we can seek God and ask Him to place upon our heart a vision for how we should work, or a vision for how our team, department, or even the whole organisation, should work. As John Carr has said, 'All God's people should be men and women of vision.'[1] Vision will help motivate us and focus our efforts and energy in the right place, to achieve the right priorities. It will help stretch and develop us in a God-orientated direction. Without vision, there is little scope for us to move forward. With vision, and with action consistent with the vision, God can do great things through us.

A LEADER PEOPLE FOLLOWED

Joseph provides an excellent model of leadership for Christians in the workplace. Peter Curran has helped to clarify what leadership is all about:

> Leading involves bringing vision and direction, motivating, enabling and caring for others, stewarding resources and making decisions. To do this in a Christian way, through serving, means leading by example, valuing the opinion of others, being willing to

---

[1] See J. Carr, *Vision*, Charis Publications 1989

sacrifice one's own desires for the benefit of others, not being obsessed with one's own status or position, wanting others to grow and flourish, and protecting them from harm, through self-sacrifice if necessary. It requires characteristics such as trustworthiness, fairness, humility, faith, obedience, wisdom, self discipline, perseverance and openness to God.[1]

Joseph brought the vision and direction as to how things should be managed during the famine. He led the campaign wisely, requiring people to pay for grain, losing their livestock—and even losing land when the livestock had gone. Although his plan might sound harsh, he thereby ensured that they accepted some responsibility for their lives. This was going to be vitally important if they were to rise up and rebuild the nation's prosperity after the famine. Had he encouraged the people to be dependent, it is possible that their desire to succeed and take responsibility for their future would have diminished. Joseph enabled them in this re-building work, encouraging them to be self-sufficient by releasing to them the seed they would need to plant in order to raise a crop after the famine. It was their responsibility to do the re-building, and Joseph did not take that away by making the people dependent through free handouts during the famine. He led the programme in a way that helped them stand on their feet with dignity during and after the crisis. This was wise leadership. He led the programme in a way that was best for his boss (as Pharaoh prospered greatly from the sale of grain); best for the people, and best for the nation in the long run. His actions had reinforced more fundamental values, though it was harder for the people in the short-term. The strategy could so easily have made him unpopular, and people could have resented his methods. However, his was a wise and winning way; his strategy, and its implementation, exhibited real leadership.

Joseph's plan helped ensure the long-term prosperity of the nation. When he gave the people the seed for planting, he established the policy that they were required to bring a fifth of their crop to Pharaoh. Hence he encouraged the people to be self-sufficient in generating wealth, but also to be responsible for the general welfare of the nation as a whole. His actions were

---

[1] *Op. cit.*, pp. 190–191

underpinned by clear values—the hallmark of a leader.

The people followed Joseph's plan. They had no alternative. He had won their support, respect and honour by the way he led. He outlined the strategy very clearly, and they knew exactly where they stood. How many leaders of companies are criticised for poor communication to their employees? ('Where are we going? No one tells us anything around here....') During the famine it was made absolutely clear that they had to pay for the grain. Amidst the confusion and chaos, the message was communicated clearly, and was clearly understood by the people. During times of crisis or change, communication from those in leadership positions in organisations can all too often become confused, insufficient and ineffective. As we have noted, there was no corruption in Joseph's life. He did not stash the money away for himself. Power did not make him proud and arrogant. Because he led with authority, wisdom and integrity, they followed him as a credible leader whom they could trust. Because he presented himself as the man in charge, they followed him. Because he worked hard for the success of the strategy and made himself visible to the people by being involved, they followed him—and even honoured him. Because he communicated clearly to people, they flowed with the vision and the strategy.

A FRUITFUL VINE IN A BARREN PLACE

Egypt was a spiritually barren land, a heathen nation, and into this land had come Joseph, an immigrant boy with neither worldly possessions nor status. But this was not the first time Joseph had been brought into a barren situation. His mother, Rachel, had been unable to conceive a child for Jacob for many years until God enabled her to do so. The arrival of Joseph took away the disgrace of her barrenness. While Joseph had nothing in terms of wealth, possessions or status when he entered Egypt, God was with him; He enabled and prospered him. Just as Joseph had been given the name 'he shall add' when Rachel bore him, so God added to him. From a humble position, God promoted him to high government office, and he prospered materially. God also gave him a family, and when he named his second son

Ephraim, Joseph declared, 'It is because God has made me fruitful in the land of my suffering' (Genesis 41:52). By positioning and blessing Joseph in such an arid place, God demonstrated that His power alone could bring life, hope, prosperity and blessing. Not only was Joseph blessed, he was also a channel of blessing to others. God made him fruitful. Reunited with his family, he blessed them by settling them in the best land of Egypt. Through the famine relief strategy, Joseph was able to ensure the continued fruitfulness of Egypt and surrounding nations. The nations became fruitful again as he provided the seed they needed to restore food production. As a result of his work, a remnant of God's people was preserved—and the line of descent to Jesus. As the roots of this man's life were sunk deep into God, and deep into God's purpose and plan, he rose up like a fruitful vine in a hard place.

God can make us fruitful in our workplaces; like Joseph, we can be fruitful vines in otherwise dry, lifeless places. If you find yourself in such a place, perhaps God has placed you there to demonstrate His power to bring change and life—so, be encouraged! By sinking your roots deeper into God, cultivating a deeper walk with Him, being open to His plan, and by working *His* way, you will see Him bless you and others. You may see souls saved where you work, godly people established in positions of power, and positive change. Your company can be blessed and be more successful just because you work there. Prayer is the starting point. We can ask God to do things through us that will be a blessing to others and a testimony throughout eternity. Why not pray along the following lines:

Lord, I don't want to live a mediocre life with nothing to show for it. I want You to do something good through my life. I have seen the marvellous things You did through people like Joseph and Daniel; Lord, I ask You to sink the roots of my working life into You and into Your plan. Establish me and make me a fruitful vine where I am. Bless the people and this company, and bring glory to Your Name, I pray. Lead me on in Your purpose and plan.

SUMMARY OF KEY POINTS

1. Joseph lived in a world which was hostile and alien to the ways of God—and so do we. The character of Joseph provides a model of a worker, from which we can learn. For example, he maintained a standard of excellence in the face of injustice, hostility and adversity, and he utilised his skills, potential and talents to the full.

2. The account of Joseph also illustrates the profound fact that God can be at work through our working life. While God will not have the same plan and purpose for us as He had for Joseph, if we walk with Him, consistently and carefully, then God can use our working life to have an impact on the world. The impact He can have through us is far greater than we imagine.

QUESTIONS FOR REFLECTION/DISCUSSION

1. Read Proverbs 19:21 and Psalm 33:11. Looking back over your life—and particularly your working life so far—what purpose and plan can you see in the way God has worked in the ups and downs and changes you have faced?

2. What are some of the main lessons that you have learned about how to successfully live out your Christian life in the workplace?

3. Paul encouraged Christians to 'eagerly desire spiritual gifts' (1 Corinthians 14:1). Which gifts of the spirit do you think could have most impact in your workplace, if used wisely?

4. Taking the gifts of prophecy and the 'word of knowledge' as examples, in what practical ways could these gifts be useful in your workplace? How would these gifts need to be used wisely to be beneficial?

5. Think about someone you regard as a good leader at work. What is it about them, and about the way they think and behave, that makes them a good leader?

6. In what sense do you consider your workplace to be a godly or an ungodly place?

7. What is it about Joseph's character and approach to working that you could most usefully learn from and apply yourself?

8. List the ways in which anything from this chapter or from your review of the above questions applies to you as a working person in your own circumstances. Then list any **actions** you will take as a result of this study (e.g. further study or reflection, prayer, speaking to someone, requests for help, changing something about yourself) and be as specific as possible about **when** you will complete the action(s).

11

'CHANGE'—FRIEND OR FOE?

A business magazine recently carried an article about an order of nuns who called in consultants to help them save their failing care-home enterprise. It was clear that radical change was needed to take them from where they were (using outdated and inefficient practices) to where they needed to be to survive as a viable enterprise. Basic business practices were introduced, as well as formal structures. Sisters became line managers in charge of care units, and received management skills training. Initially, however, some nuns were hostile to the changes, and one refused to attend the training sessions. The life that had been in many ways so familiar and predictable became very different and the nuns entered a world they had never experienced before. Their account illustrates many of the difficulties and challenges associated with change. Sometimes change is inevitable or necessary if we are going to move on to better things. Change can also be imposed from the outside, and it often requires us to make an emotional adjustment, which can be difficult and even painful. It often means that we are forced out of our comfort zone of routine and familiarity and have to step forward into something unfamiliar. We constantly have to deal with change in the workplace.

As Christians, we should be no strangers to change because

God Himself is in the business of changing us. He uses our daily experiences, including our work, to change us for the better, to help us become more like Jesus. Difficulties, trials, events, activities, and our experiences with people, can help remould and reshape us. Our experiences can help us cultivate new qualities or skills, maturing us as Christians. Through changes in our circumstances, God can move our lives in a different direction and lead us on to new things that we would probably not have chosen, but which will be the best for us. These events or experiences can be sudden (redundancy or change of job) or long-term and gradual (working closely with a difficult colleague), and may or may not seem pleasant at the time. If we choose to respond positively, then as the potter's hand works to change us through our experience of working life, we can indeed be changed to reflect more of Christ. We can also become more fulfilled in the work we do, as we go with the flow of God's purpose and plan for our life.

We are called to be 'salt' and 'light' to the world around us. Salt brings taste and flavour to an otherwise bland or mundane experience. Light completely transforms the darkness, so that people can see something they otherwise could not see. Both salt and light bring a change that makes a positive difference. We should make a difference in the workplace. Not only are we ourselves to be changed, we are also to be used by God to bring change.

Our attitude towards change will affect how quickly and how far we change for the better, and how open we are to being used as an instrument of change in the world around us. We can resist change in ourselves, preferring to carry on in our 'comfort zone' and we can choose to continue in a rut. We can also respond to change with fear, denial or hostility. If we resist change, then we are not likely to reach the same maturity in Christ as quickly or be as successful and fulfilled in our work as if we embrace change as a positive challenge, or even as an opportunity. Being open to positive change in ourselves, and seeking to bring positive change in the world of work around us, may not be the most comfortable position for us to be in and it may not be our normal or preferred way of living. But as champions for God in the workplace, change should be our friend rather than our enemy.

EMBRACING CHANGE

For many in the working world, the only thing that has been constant for the last few years has been change. Changes in working practices, technology, organisational structures and culture have, for many of us, become part of life. Here are a few headlines taken from the recent business press, illustrating the kinds of changes that are now commonplace:

- ☐ **'Parting company'** —a review of recent de-mergers which resulted in job losses for many people. As for the employees who kept their jobs in one company, 'many of them felt a sense of mourning for departing colleagues, with some expressing feelings of guilt'. There was a strong emotional response to a sudden change over which people had no control.

- ☐ **'High-Performance Working'** —a case study of a century old brewing company that in the last ten years has implemented a programme of global expansion, innovation and performance improvement, to radically increase production and market share. Employees had to adapt to new company values, a new vision and team working. Their jobs were also redesigned, and they had to learn new skills and demonstrate different attitudes from those that had previously been acceptable. There were also fewer jobs now.

- ☐ **'High time for action'** —an article that highlighted an increasing incidence of drug and alcohol addiction and drug abuse at work.

- ☐ **'Merger sparks redundancy fears'** —as well as predictions of up to five thousand job losses in a major pharmaceutical company, there are doubts about the future of two UK research plants. Where there was once a 'jobs for life' culture there is lingering uncertainty about the longer-term.

- ☐ **'Ascent of woman'** —a review of the emerging trend for more women to be found in positions of leadership in business. The author of the article made the following prediction: 'I believe that women's advancement is virtually unstoppable. Women will be the ones running the world in a hundred years' time.'

☐ '**Instrumental change**' —This article describes how a company manufacturing medical devices sought to improve efficiency and performance. Part of the programme of improvement involved a more disciplined approach to working. Late delivery was no longer tolerated and staff were encouraged to question the way things were done rather than just accept the old ways. This required a change of mind-set and behaviour, and some were not able to accept and adapt to the new ways.

These brief examples illustrate the kinds of changes many of us will have experienced, or will experience, as well as the emotional and psychological responses associated with change. Some people lose jobs, and the new ways of doing business require different skills, attitudes and values. Such changes can make us uncomfortable, anxious or even stressed; and adapting to something new can require courage, flexibility and a willingness to move on. But resisting change, ignoring it or denying the need for it in ourselves only makes the process of moving forward more difficult, slower and more stressful. We have to get used to doing things differently, or get left behind—or, worse still, left out.

As we have suggested, Christians should be familiar with change. Change for good should not be an alien threat to us, but rather a healthy part of our Christian walk—something we embrace. First of all, when we accept Jesus as our Saviour, there is transformation in us. We are made righteous by the blood of Jesus; we are forgiven, and reconciled to God as His sons and daughters. We are given access to the Father, and He comes to live in us by His Spirit. We have a living relationship with God and get to know Him through Jesus. As we move on in our Christian walk, God works in us to change our heart, character and attitudes. A healthy Christian life is really all about change, some sudden and radical, some more incremental. If we are open to God working in us, then we should also be open to change. Only God does not change; everything else is subject to His change programme, including you and me.

Secondly, God tends to bring change into our life when He wants to move us on in His purpose and plan. Whilst we may not understand it at the time, it will be a positive thing in the life of a Christian who walks with the Lord. We have noted the tremendous changes Joseph experienced, and which were necessary so that he would be fruitful. We recall, too, that God changed Abram's name to Abraham, which means 'father of many', emphasising that through this one man He would change the course of history. God changed Saul, a persecutor of Christians, to Paul, a soul winner for God—change by means of a dramatic conversion.

While some changes, such as redundancy, can be painful, if we are open to the Lord He can work something out for good. In such circumstances we may need to hold on to the truth of God's word in faith, patience and perseverance, but reminding ourselves that,

> ...in all things God works for the good of those who love him, who have been called according to his purpose.
>
> *Romans 8:28*

Thirdly, as we noted, God does not want us to be in a rut, but to fulfil the potential that we have and His plan for our life. He brings about new things and new beginnings as well as strengthening and reinforcing the good things of the past or present. A rut, therefore, is not a place we should be in for too long. Change can be healthy, a way that God expands, stretches and develops us; and as we walk in His ways and embrace positive change, He can lead us on to whole new chapters in our life.

Reflecting upon his successful career, Don Latham, has noted:

> ...another lesson I was to learn is that God does not want us in a rut. We may have to wait for the next thing to be prepared, but God wants us to use and develop our talents and abilities.... God does not want us to find security in a rut. God is most interested in our personal development and our relationship with Him.[1]

Of course, not every change in the world of work is necessarily good. For example, New Age philosophy has found its way into

---

[1] D. Latham, *A Faith that Works*, Terra Nova Publications, 1997

some management training courses and, as we have noted, there is a greater incidence of drug abuse in the workplace nowadays. Naturally, these are changes we should reject and resist as Christians. Our willingness to embrace positive change will affect how far we reach the potential that God has put in us.

BEING CHANGED

A British missionary who spent many years in Indonesia, and saw many people accept Christ, said he went there expecting to change the country. Several years after he returned, he was able to see that through his missionary experience it had been more the case that God had taken him to Indonesia to change him. God is very interested in who we are, and His plan for us is that we should be changed to be more like Jesus:

> ...for those God foreknew he also predestined to be conformed to the likeness of his Son, that he might be the firstborn among many brothers.
>
> *Romans 8:29*

God's change agenda for each of us does not involve just learning a new repertoire of outward behaviour as an overlay to who we are underneath. It is not about learning a set of stock Christian phrases. His agenda is about transforming us; and only He can do it, by His Spirit and His word working in us. When we are born again, God creates a new spirit within us. The regenerated person has different attitudes, values, thought patterns and behaviour, as the Holy Spirit sanctifies us, and as the mind receives and applies the word of God. Some of the changes which God wants to make in us are listed below.

As we progressively choose to focus our mind on godly things, and choose to follow His ways in moments when we are drawn to sin, then our mind will be renewed; godliness will be reflected in our attitudes, speech and actions. As we give control of every area of our life to Him, and ask His Spirit to work in us, He will build in us the character of Christ, leading us on to maturity. He will put us through the experiences we need, to change us in the way that He wants. Some experiences will be pleasant, some more difficult, but as we yield to His work in our life, He will work out His plan.

GOD'S CHANGE AGENDA FOR YOU

CHANGED FROM...

Those who live according to the sinful nature have their minds set on what that nature desires.

Romans 8:5

The mind of the sinful man is death

Romans 8:6

...the sinful mind is hostile to God. It does not submit to God's law, nor can it do so.

Romans 8:7

A desire to glorify self, and to seek high position and profile

"What do you want me to do for you?" he asked.
They replied, "Let one of us sit at your right and the other at your left in your glory."

Mark 10:36–37

...sexual immorality, impurity and debauchery; idolatry and witchcraft; hatred, discord, jealousy, fits of rage, selfish ambition, dissentions, factions and envy; drunkenness, orgies, and the like.

Galatians 5:19–21

'Lording' it over other people, and abuse of power

"You know that those who are regarded as rulers of the Gentiles lord it over them, and their high officials exercise authority over them."

Mark 10:42

Pride goes before destruction, a haughty spirit before a fall.

Proverbs 16:18

A hot-tempered man stirs up dissension....'

Proverbs 15:18

CHANGED TO...

...but those who live in accordance with the Spirit have their minds set on what the Spirit desires.

Romans 8:5

...but the mind controlled by the Spirit is life and peace.

Romans 8:6

Now the Lord is the Spirit, and where the Spirit of the Lord is, there is freedom.

2 Corinthians 3:17

And we, who with unveiled faces all reflect the Lord's glory, are being transformed into his likeness with ever-increasing glory, which comes from the Lord, who is the Spirit.

2 Corinthians 3:18

Be joyful in hope, patient in affliction, faithful in prayer. Share with God's people who are in need. Practise hospitality.

Romans 12:12–13

Bless those who persecute you; bless and do not curse.

Romans 12:14

May he strengthen your hearts so that you will be blameless and holy in the presence of our God and Father when our Lord Jesus comes with all his holy ones.

1 Thessalonians 3:13

Live in harmony with one another. Do not be proud, but be willing to associate with people of low position. Do not be conceited.

Romans 12:16

Do not repay anyone evil for evil. Be careful to do what is right in the eyes of everybody. If it is possible, as far as it depends on you, live in peace with everyone. Do not take revenge, my friends....

Romans 12:17–19

Everyone must submit himself to the governing authorities, for there is no authority except that which God has established.

Romans 13:1

"Not so with you. Instead, whoever wants to become great among you must be your servant."

Mark 10:43

Do nothing out of selfish ambition or vain conceit, but in humility consider others better than yourselves. Each of you should look not only to his own interests, but also to the interests of others.

Philippians 2:3,4

Do everything without complaining or arguing, so that you may become blameless and pure, children of God without fault in a crooked and depraved generation, in which you shine like stars in the universe.

Philippians 2:14–15

But the fruit of the Spirit is love, joy, peace, patience, kindness, goodness, faithfulness, gentleness and self-control.

Galatians 5:22–23

Be kind and compassionate to one another, forgiving each other, just as in Christ God forgave you.

Ephesians 4:32

The lips of the wise spread knowledge....

Proverbs 15:7

Working life brings all kinds of pressures, difficulties, disappointments, struggles and challenges as well as successes. Through all these circumstances, God can highlight our need to be changed, and move us on in His change agenda. James celebrated the positive impact of trials and difficulties on the development of our Christian character:

Consider it pure joy, my brothers, whenever you face trials of many kinds, because you know that the testing of your faith develops perseverance. Perseverance must finish its work so that you may be mature and complete, not lacking anything.

James 1:2–4

CHAMPIONS FOR GOD AT WORK

The hand of the master potter can be at work as we work, bringing us through the events and circumstances we need to go through, so that He can get us to where He wants us to be. He can break our pride, for example, by bringing us through circumstances over which we seem to have little influence or control. He can nurture compassion in us, as well as the ability to feel empathy with others as we experience injustice or difficult circumstances. He can bring us to a new level of faith and trust in Him as we face uncertainty and experience insecurity in our job circumstances. He can help us to relate to others more effectively as we rub shoulders with difficult people or as we are forced to collaborate with others. He can show us our rebellious streak as we work for an incompetent or unreasonable boss. As He allows us to go through the pressure and heat of difficult circumstances, He can make us tougher, more robust, resilient and sharper—a more effective instrument in His hands.

Here are just some of the circumstances you can face at work:

☐ injustice in the face of your good conduct and conscientious work;

☐ being passed over for promotion when you feel that you are clearly the best;

☐ your good work going unrecognised, or being credited to others;

☐ events or decisions that seem to work against your best interests;

☐ working with a difficult boss or colleague(s);

☐ disappointments, such as not getting the pay rise you expected and feel you deserve;

☐ mistreatment by others;

☐ making mistakes, and having to deal with the consequences of your mistakes;

☐ times of uncertainty over your future, job security or income;

☐ temptations, such as to be dishonest or compromise your Christian standards;

☐ experience of redundancy;

172

- ☐   a change of boss who brings new standards and demands;
- ☐   a change of responsibilities and work role; and,
- ☐   facing a task or challenge which is beyond your ability and skill.

When you face such difficulties, the Lord could well be at work—changing you. As He works in our daily lives to change us, it is important that we remain close to Him. We need to be willing to be changed. To maintain such a positive attitude will certainly require faith. Redundancy, for example, can feel like the end of the world. However, if we maintain a clear belief that God is in control, and that He is working things out for good, then we will be strong enough to persevere. If not, then change will be a threat and feel like an enemy.

If we are going to be changed, we need to be able to learn from our experiences and mistakes. However painful it might be, we need to be learners. Through the prophet Isaiah, God encouraged His people to be learners: 'learn to do right!' (Isaiah 1:17).

During his successful career in local government, Don Latham had to learn some hard lessons from his mistakes. Once, he failed to get a job that seemed to be in God's plan, because he had not been open to God's leading and had not taken practical steps to prepare himself for the interview. He missed opportunities and blessings, but learned from his mistakes and got it right next time. Successful people are not those who have never made any mistakes. They have learned to pick themselves up after a setback, put it behind them, and carry on. They are the people who have reflected on their experiences, and have learned lessons from them—and this helps them to perform better next time.

Personal change also involves learning and developing new skills, and addressing our 'weaknesses' or 'development needs'. If God's standard for all of us is excellence then we have a responsibility to develop ourselves—to meet the demands of the work, and prepare ourselves to move on further in His career development plan for our life. We are to be like those in the parable of the talents who took proactive steps to put to work the gifts that they had been given, and who were rewarded. Here are some of the practical steps we can take to develop ourselves, and to multiply our talents:

☐ Take the initiative to get the training and education you need.

☐ Seek out new assignments and take on new responsibilities (following any necessary preparation).

☐ Find ways to work with the best people—people who you can learn something from.

☐ Ask questions.

☐ Take on a more stretching assignment, a new challenge or something completely different.

☐ Take time to read relevant books and journals to keep up to date, and to develop greater awareness, knowledge and understanding.

☐ Persevere to develop new skills and capabilities—being prepared to learn from mistakes along the way.

☐ Try to find out, and write down, what sort of behaviour and attitudes your boss seems to value in people. Check how you match these, and identify how you need to change (in ways that are consistent with being a Christian.)

☐ Try to get an accurate picture of your own strengths and weaknesses. Ask for feedback from your manager; be clear about how you need to improve.

☐ Try to identify why you are not progressing in your career as much as you might wish or expect to; face up to the issues, and try to deal with whatever is holding you back.

☐ Draw up a career and personal development plan, setting out how you plan to address your development needs and get the skills required to achieve your aspirations.

☐ Regularly review your progress in terms of your development plan, and take steps to make it happen.

☐ Try to learn as much as possible from all assignments and jobs you are given. Take time to reflect on what you have learned, and write it down.

☐ Try to excel in everything that is set before you, however menial the job may be. Sometimes it is the tasks which do not seem important to us, or the fine details in what we do, that really matter to those in positions of authority over us.

☐ Be open to changing your employer, or your role within the company, to broaden your experience base—and seek God's leading on this.

☐ Ask God to open up relevant doors and opportunities for you to get relevant experience, and to close those doors that He does not want you to go through.

MAKING CHANGE

Some time ago, I boarded a busy commuter train in Singapore and sat opposite a youth whose t. shirt carried the message 'Make Change' in large, bold letters. A simple statement, but making or promoting change in the secular workplace can be tough, requiring courage and determination. There are others' reactions and emotions to deal with. When Stephen preached the gospel to the Jews, and when the Lord did miraculous things through him, there was opposition. The gospel of grace required change for those steeped in the Law. They did not like the fact that they had to change, and Stephen experienced the backlash of their anger. Nehemiah faced opposition from those who did not want him to succeed. People generally do not like to see change around them if they are comfortable with the status quo; and the devil does not like change when it means the kingdom of God advances. But therein lies the challenge for us as champions for God at work —to bring God inspired change to the world around us, even when the world does not want to embrace it.

Wherever we work and whatever we do, there are at least three ways in which our workplace could probably change for the better. Firstly, there may be room for positive change in the way work is organised and conducted. Is there a healthy balance between the needs of the workforce and the priority given to efficiency and delivery? Schumacher has argued that if an employer places too much emphasis on efficiency, then some of the more fulfilling aspects of the work can disappear. His belief is that people find it more rewarding if they are responsible, as far as possible, for the whole of the work process rather than for a small part of it. He also believes that such an approach is more consistent with a godly approach to work. In your workplace, are people organised in a way that encourages conflict or co-operation? How high are the standards for the quality of work, and how well are the standards communicated to those doing the work? Is there a healthy balance between the focus on immediate work delivery and the need to develop people and processes to ensure longer term improvement and success? Are working practices honest, and is integrity valued? Are resources wasted? Is there a vision for where the organisation is going, and a strategy for getting there? Are there small improvements that you can make to whatever work you do?

Secondly, there may be scope for positive change in people's experience of working life. Do staff feel rewarded and recognised for doing good work? Are those in positions of power listening to the workforce? Is the behaviour and attitude of those in authority consistent with the expressed values of the organisation (e.g. 'our people are our greatest asset')? Is there an atmosphere of trust? Are people caught up in petty feuds and power struggles? Do managers communicate with staff, actively develop them, and encourage them to develop themselves? Are people thanked in a natural way for doing good work?

Thirdly, there will be scope for change in the spiritual lives of the people who work in the organisation. What are the common areas of sin and compromise? What struggles do people have both inside and outside work? Is there a Christian witness in the workplace?

When we stop to reflect, the potential for positive change in the world around us is enormous. So how can we play our part in making it happen?

We can challenge the working standards of the world and the way work is done, by the way we choose to work and by the way we encourage others to work. As we work to an excellent standard, whatever others do, we can affect the quality of work produced and the material success of the organisation. We can show people that we are committed to working well whether we are rewarded and recognised or not. We choose to work well because we work for God.

We can try to be more creative and innovative in our work and encourage this style of working in other people. Creative thinking is about developing new ideas, and new ideas can bring positive change and benefit. However, research such as that of Michael West has shown that most organisations give relatively little space or support to creativity. One exception is 3M where technical staff are encouraged to spend 15% of their time on their own ideas and projects in the hope that at least some of them may generate a useful product for the company. Most of us probably do not work in such a supportive environment. The team, management style and general working culture of your organisation may not support or encourage creative thinking that will bring about useful change. People can be critical, cynical, and can feel threatened by new ideas. This can block the very creativity the business might need. Even if we have a new idea, there is then a need for innovation—which is all about implementing the idea in the practical context. Again, people can resist the implementation of new ideas, and team dynamics can discourage progress. We may need to persevere to see innovation, just like the man from 3M who invented the yellow post-it notes. He sang in the church choir and needed some effective way of marking the place of hymns, between services. Knowing of an adhesive with poor properties (it didn't stick well) which was being investigated within the company, he had the idea of using it on small strips of paper to mark the hymnal. But the real innovation came with his persistence in selling the idea to secretaries, chief executives, the marketing department and the sales department in the organisation. It is now a two hundred million dollar business for 3M.

We can be 'salt' and 'light' to people around us and have a positive impact on their experience of work. Kind words and small acts of kindness can help. Looking after the welfare and development of the people for whom we are responsible will be appreciated. Communicating with others in a way that shows respect and empathy will make them feel valued—and it is likely that many around you, rightly or wrongly, do not feel valued.

Finally, we must go on praying, as God is the only One who can bring change of eternal significance into peoples' lives. The way things are done in the place where you work can reflect a variety of influences, such as the personality of the leader, its historical roots, and even the influence of demonic powers or 'strongholds'. We can see consistent patterns of cruelty, pride, criticism, dishonesty, fear and conflict in relationships and working practices. But the Lord can make a difference when we pray for change in the spiritual realms over our workplaces, and in the lives of people. Both Daniel and Nehemiah prayed for change, earnestly asking God to restore Jerusalem from desolation. They had a vision for positive change, and turned that into prayer.

Here are some of the lessons we can learn from their prayers for change:

Their prayers began worshipfully and acknowledged the sovereignty of God over the particular circumstances and problems that they saw.
Daniel prayed: 'O Lord, the great and awesome God, who keeps his covenant of love with all who love him and obey his commands' (Daniel 9:4). Nehemiah began his prayer in a similar way: 'O Lord, God of heaven, the great and awesome God, who keeps his covenant of love with those who love him and obey his commands' (Nehemiah 1:5).

They humbly acknowledged the sin of the people before God—as sin was the root of the problems.
Daniel prayed, 'we have sinned and done wrong. We have been wicked and have rebelled; we have turned away from your commands and laws. We have not listened to your servants the prophets, who spoke in your name to our kings, our princes and our fathers, and to all the people of the land' (Daniel 9:5–6). Nehemiah similarly interceded for the sins of the people and confessed his own sin: 'I confess the sins we Israelites, including myself and my father's house, have committed against you. We have acted very wickedly toward you. We have not obeyed the commands, decrees and laws you gave your servant Moses' (Nehemiah 1:6–7).

They acknowledged God as being a merciful and covenant keeping God, able to deal with the problems that they saw.
Daniel appealed, 'O Lord, in keeping with all your righteous acts, turn away your anger and your wrath from Jerusalem, your city, your holy hill' (Daniel 9:16). Nehemiah appealed to the God who keeps His word: 'Remember the instruction you gave your servant Moses, saying, "If you are unfaithful, I will scatter you among the nations, but if you return to me and obey my commands, then even if your exiled people are at the farthest horizon, I will gather them from there and bring them to the place I have chosen as a dwelling for my Name"' (Nehemiah 1:8–9).

They asked God to do something about the problem and to bring real change.

Daniel asked God to restore His sanctuary: 'Now, our God, hear the prayers and petitions of your servant. For your sake, O Lord, look with favour on your desolate sanctuary' (Daniel 9:17). Nehemiah asked Him that he might find favour with his boss—to release him to go to Jerusalem to begin the building work: 'O Lord, let your ear be attentive to the prayer of this your servant and to the prayer of your servants who delight in revering your name. Give your servant success today by granting him favour in the presence of this man' (Nehemiah 1:11). God answered.

As we work to God's standard, as we are 'salt' and 'light' to those around us in the workplace, and as we pray for change, God can unravel His change agenda for our workplace through us. We are not in our workplace by accident. It may feel like it, but God is in control. He has a plan and purpose to touch your workplace through you. To co-operate in God's change agenda will require faith, courage and perseverance on our part, as well as dependence upon His grace, but when we come face to face with Him, how good it will sound when He says, 'Well done my good and faithful servant.'

SUMMARY OF KEY POINTS

1. Our experiences in the world of work can be instrumental in changing us for the better. God can use our work experience to mature us, put new qualities and abilities in us and make us more like Jesus. We should, therefore, embrace change positively, bravely and boldly, making the most of every opportunity that God opens up for us.

2. As Christians, we can have a positive effect on the people we work with, and on the atmosphere and culture of the organisation we work for, and its working practices. The more we allow God to work in us and through us, the greater our potential will be to have a positive impact.

QUESTIONS FOR REFLECTION/DISCUSSION

1. From your consideration of the following verses, what are some of the main reasons why people resist change?

   - Matthew 12:1–14
   - Matthew 15:1–14
   - Matthew 22:34–40
   - John 6:41–42
   - John 11:45–48
   - Acts 4:13–22

2. What are some of the changes you have experienced at work? How have you and others responded to them, and what impact have they had on you?

3. How has your experience of working life changed you?

4. What are some of the practical steps you can take to develop your skills in a way that will help you at work?

5. What are some of the ways in which your workplace needs to change for the better?

6. What are some of the practical steps you could take to help make a difference in your workplace and change things for the better?

7. If you were to start praying for change in your workplace, or in the lives of the people you work with, what specific things would you pray for?

8. List the ways in which anything from this chapter or from your review of the above questions applies to you as a working person in your own circumstances. Then list any **actions** you will take as a result of this study (e.g. further study or reflection, prayer, speaking to someone, requests for help, changing something about yourself) and be as specific as possible about **when** you will complete the action(s).

12

PAY OR NO PAY

Pay is not the defining characteristic of 'work'. Work is about serving through your labour, not specifically about money or job titles. 'Homemakers' work very hard, doing the shopping, looking after children, doing the low profile housework and generally supporting the rest of the family in a whole variety of ways. Try telling busy homemakers that they are not workers! They may not get paid for it, but they *serve through their labour*, and in that sense they work, though it is usually to support others who go out and earn the money. Whole groups of the population are not being paid, but are nonetheless serving through their labour—including full-time parents, voluntary workers and the retired. The unemployed can also be 'workers', though they are usually regarded as 'out of work', or 'in between jobs'. But there is a strong tendency for us to regard pay as the defining feature of work, and the amount of pay and prestige associated with a particular job as the measure of its importance. So unpaid workers often feel undervalued.

Whether or not we are paid for our work, the important thing for us all is to be good stewards both of our time and whatever resources have been entrusted to us. Our aim should be to do something useful rather than be idle, and to do it in a Christ-like way, as a worship offering to God. We are called to do excellent work whether we are looking after the home and supporting the family or working as the Chief Executive of a large corporation. Our satisfaction should come from working for God and doing it His way, not from the size of our pay cheque or from our job title. Our self-esteem should come from a clear understanding of who we are in Christ, rather than from the status or position that we attain in our job or career.

HOMEMAKERS

A recent look at a typical issue of one of the more 'conservative' magazines aimed at family-orientated women homemakers was revealing. There were useful features on dealing with sleep problems, and how to organise the home to make best use of available space. There were useful tips for improving the garden, and plenty of suggestions for family holidays. However, the majority of the magazine suggested that there is a national obsession with food for pleasure, and also shows the huge importance people give to their personal appearance. Some 40% of the magazine space was devoted to articles about food and recipes, whilst over 30% of the magazine space showed clothes and beauty enhancement products, as well as features dealing with how to stay looking young. These were some of the other features, which betrayed the worldly values and preoccupations that must seem entirely normal to many homemakers: an article strongly advocating the wisdom and value of letting your unmarried children have sex with their partners in your home; how to get the ideal fake sun tan; a review of a filmstar's three broken marriages—and why she now lives with a man who is fifteen years younger than herself; case studies of women who leave their husbands and children to go on holiday alone; how a beauty treatment helps a woman look refreshed and radiant throughout the day, and gives her confidence; as well as articles dealing with the occult.

There were, however, six column inches tucked away in this 100-page magazine that reflected something of the reality and challenges of being a homemaker. It featured a 'house-husband', a man in his forties who had taken on the role of homemaker, looking after the household affairs as well as two young children, while his wife worked in paid employment. He observed that other dads were envious when they discovered he was a house-husband, but that they would think differently if they knew how hard it was. A tough job, with little obvious extrinsic reward, home-making demands self-sacrifice and patience, as well as a servant heart—and plenty of sheer hard work. Without the hard work, dedication and commitment of the homemaker, the family could not function. Such a job demands the stuff that champions are made of.

The writer of Proverbs paints for us a portrait of a wife and homemaker with very different values, standards and concerns from those reflected in the magazine. She is a model wife and a model worker in all she does, working to God's standards in her service to her family. She works to the same standard of excellence as, for example, Daniel and Joseph in their senior civil service jobs in Babylon and Egypt. Her life and her work are valuable and significant. Working as a homemaker may seem to be a low profile job, and homemakers can sometimes feel insignificant, particularly as they are not working for an immediate and measurable reward, like money. Consequently, it is hard to place a 'value' on their work. Many women choose not to do it and prefer—or, perhaps, need—to work in paid employment. Homemaking may not be regarded as a high status role, even among Christians. It can also be a difficult role, as homemakers can feel they get taken for granted and are not fully appreciated. Sometimes hard work may not be obvious. I remember coming home after work one day, soon after I was married, and asked my wife what she had done all day. She said she had vacuum cleaned the house, and I remember thinking to myself, 'Is that all!' But I soon realised what effort it took when I had to clean the house a few days later. I discovered the vacuum cleaner was so old, inefficient and broken that it took hours on bended knees to do the job, though my wife had never complained—as, indeed, she never does. I was truly humbled. Sometimes we men do not realise the hard work involved in keeping the home running smoothly, especially when the children come along. I discovered, too, that it is far easier to go to work than to stay at home and look after pre-school children!

The woman in Proverbs serves her family by working with all her heart and energy. She looks after them, making sure the household runs smoothly and efficiently for the good of the family. Through her excellent hard work and her godly qualities, she brings honour to her husband and to God. As a result she is 'worth far more than rubies' (Proverbs 31:10) and deserves a reward as well as public praise:

> Give her the reward she has earned, and let her works bring her praise at the city gate.
>
> *Proverbs 31:31*

The woman is valuable and precious in God's eyes. We read that, 'She watches over the affairs of her household and does not eat the bread of idleness' (Proverbs 31:27). She knows her responsibility is to look after the household and family affairs, and she consistently gives her best effort, focusing upon the important tasks that keep the family going. She is no sluggard; she does not concern herself with finding the perfect dress, or with staying young looking. Instead she gets up early to prepare food for the family and the servants. She makes coverings for her bed, and plans ahead to ensure the family have the clothes they need, even if the weather should suddenly change. She is highly motivated and gets on with the practical work she faces. There is a real sense of personal fulfilment in the way she works with 'eager hands' to make cloth, and in how she sets about her work 'vigorously'. Like Daniel, there is no evidence of negligence or corruption in her working life. Instead she delivers excellent work, day in, day out. We find that she brings her husband good, 'all the days of her life' (Proverbs 31:12). She does not spend her time planning holidays away from her family so she can enjoy independence. She does not let boredom or frustration get the better of her. She gets on with doing a good job, because she knows that is what God wants her to do.

While she serves in the home, she is also resourceful and industrious enough to find ways to contribute to the family income. She is a shrewd businesswoman, who 'considers' a field before buying it. She is not rash, impulsive or naïve in her business dealings. With the earnings she makes from her investment in the field, she invests in a vineyard which brings a longer-term and regular source of income and benefit for the family. She weighs things up before she invests, to make sure it is a sound investment. Afterwards she, '...sees that her trading is profitable' (Proverbs 31: 18). Her prudence and business acumen pays off. Similarly, she sees that there is a market for linen garments and sells them to the merchants. Making cloth and investing in property was something she could do from home in a way that did not hinder or compromise her homemaker responsibilities. This is not to say that all homemakers nowadays should be property dealers or cloth makers. However it does illustrate the point that being a homemaker need not preclude working for money too, or demonstrating a wide range of skills, abilities and interests. If the homemaker is resourceful, then he/ she may be able to contribute to the family income—just like the good wife in Proverbs.

Her godly qualities shine out. She is a woman who fears the Lord, and this is reflected in who she is and how she works. Her life as a homemaker is about pleasing and honouring her husband, the one who is placed over her as the head of the household. Just as Joseph and Daniel served their masters through their excellent work, so this woman served her husband. She brings him good rather than trouble and harm, and consequently he has full confidence in her. She is not a quarrelsome or complaining wife who is like a constantly dripping tap (Proverbs 19:13). Rather, she supports her husband in a way that wins him respect and honour—and she wins praise from her husband and children as well as from the wider community. She also shows compassion and kindness to the poor and needy. She is generous to them and provides for their needs. Even though she has earned her own money through hard work and effort, she does not condemn or dismiss the needy or judge them as 'shirkers' deserving nothing. There is no room in her life for gossip and idle chatter about fake suntans, the affairs of others, fashion or luxurious food. Instead, 'she speaks with wisdom, and faithful instruction is on her tongue' (Proverbs 31:26).

This is a woman of God, and it shows. Hers is a beauty that has nothing to do with creams, techniques for how to stay looking young, clothes or hair. Hers is a beauty that is both natural and supernatural—the goodness of God shining through her. She is a real witness to the living God by who she is, what she says, and how she works.

Not an easy role! Yet the woman in Proverbs was a fulfilled person even though she had no title or position, other than 'the wife of noble character'. Perhaps this is not an attractive work 'package' in this day and age, when many of us see our fulfilment in career terms. However, in the sight of God, she excelled: 'Many women do noble things, but you surpass them all' (Proverbs 31:29). She was a champion for God.

From a secular perspective, Loretta Kaufman and Mary Quigley have written a book to challenge the sense among women that homemaking is unimportant, boring or even something to be ashamed of.[1] They celebrate the role of what they call the 'new traditional wife', and aim to encourage women to take on the role if they can, suggesting several ways in which it can be attractive and fulfilling. It is interesting to note that at least some of the principles they suggest are to be found in the portrait of the woman of noble character described in Proverbs.

They point to four major areas that are of key importance. The first, called 'partnering', has to do with the allocation of responsibilities. Both the husband and wife play their parts in making family life work. The husband may be the primary earner, whilst the wife manages the family finances and investments, making major purchases and sales. The second area is termed 're-tooling'. The new traditional wife may use her skills, gifts and experience for the good of her community, and she may do charitable, voluntary work. Thirdly, there is the aspect of 'gift–giving'. Much satisfaction can be gained in caring for others and serving the family. Finally, there is 'back-burnering': the 'new traditional wife' may opt to work part time in order to maintain her professional skills, leaving open the possibility of going back to paid work.

THE EXPERIENCE OF 'UNEMPLOYMENT'

Research shows that the transition from paid employment to being without a paid job can be a traumatic one. Following a television news announcement that a major car plant in north

---

[1] *And What Do You Do? When Women Stay at Home*, Wildcat Canyon Press, 2000

London would close, with the loss of thousands of jobs, some of the workers interviewed were in shock as the news of closure came to them, 'like a bolt from the blue'. They found it hard to come to terms with the news and its implications. In circumstances like these, shock and disbelief are often the first reactions, which may be quickly followed by anger. Then, as unemployment becomes a reality, many people experience the loss of a sense of purpose and meaning in life. This can be accompanied by low self-esteem and the deterioration of mental and physical well-being—stress, depression, despair, and sometimes even suicide. The loss of self-esteem is perhaps not surprising when 'work' is often valued purely in terms of paid employment—and being without paid employment can carry a stigma. Self-esteem can be closely tied up with achieving success in the workplace, and our own sense of self-worth is often grounded in how much others value us—especially how much they are prepared to pay us to do a job. Peter Curran has aptly observed that the experience of unemployment, '...is made worse by a society which idolizes paid employment for its own sake or as a means to wealth, status and power.'

It is, of course, biblical for us to work if we can, to pay for the food we eat and to make every effort not to be dependent on others. It is our responsibility to work in paid employment, though some people such as homemakers can be in a supporting role for the family 'breadwinner'. However, sometimes people can find themselves out of paid employment through redundancy. As Christians, our experience of unemployment can be challenging and difficult. It may even involve some suffering. It can be a miserable and lonely experience. When I lost my job once, as a result of a cost-cutting programme, it seemed to rain every day. I could not even go out for walks as the weather was so bad—cold, wet and grey. One day, I tried to fix the garden fence with my wife's help, and as we were putting a piece of it in place I stepped backwards, accidentally putting my leg into a bucket of cold rainwater up to my knee. At that moment it felt like life could not possibly get any worse! And throughout that time I never heard any word of direction from the Lord. However, I can see with hindsight that He was working something good out for me, which involved a change of career direction. He just did it in a way that I did not expect—but then the Lord is full of surprises.

There is a way through difficult times, and God is our help, our strength, our hope, our provider, and our peace. Our life is in Him. Whilst it may be hard to appreciate sometimes, you have to remember that GOD IS IN CONTROL OF YOUR LIFE. Unemployment may be a time of testing and a time to put our trust in God, but He will work things out for good in His time and in His way:

> Trust in the Lord with all your heart and lean not on your own understanding; in all your ways acknowledge him, and he will make your paths straight.
>
> *Proverbs 3:5–6*

Besides drawing near to God, we need to have a right perspective on our experience of unemployment. We have been made in the image and likeness of God who is living and active. He has made us in His image, and so it is true to say that work is an important part of our lives. But during periods of unemployment we can find active, meaningful things to do with our time that are useful to others and fulfilling to ourselves. We can still serve through our labour even if there is no pay cheque involved. God's great works of creation have nothing to do with pay! We may need to make an effort to think of things to do, but if we look diligently, and prayerfully ask God to open doors for us to be useful, then we will be used. Searching for another job can itself be a full time job during periods away from paid employment, and if we do it to the best of our ability, then that is something worthwhile and pleasing to God. We can search for jobs, do our applications, re-train, and develop new skills with a spirit of excellence.

God has given us something meaningful and good to do. He has commissioned us to manage His created world as stewards of the earth's resources. Even if we are out of paid employment, we can still have a role in managing the earth's resources in a responsible way and to a standard of excellence. Our time and energy, as well as our money, skills and assets, are all resources. We can still use them to the best of our ability in a way that glorifies God and brings a sense of fulfilment to us. We will need to be disciplined to use our own time and talents productively, and set about working conscientiously, as our day will no longer be structured for us by our employer or workplace routines. During unemployment it is very important to plan meaningful activities, and to have clear goals and targets for what we want to achieve with our time. Staying active and maintaining a disciplined and structured use of time will help prevent boredom, apathy and aimlessness, which can lead to loss of energy and drive, depression and despair.

The Bible teaches that it is good for us to find satisfaction and pleasure in our work, and that it can be a worship offering to God. It can also bring dignity and a healthy outward focus to our lives. These are not contingent upon working for pay. If we do something useful but unpaid, and do it to a standard of excellence and in a Christ-like way, then we can still find pleasure in it. Our labours can still be an acceptable worship offering. Given our circumstances, it may also be a sacrifice of praise as we may not feel like doing voluntary work, home improvements, job applications (or even helping out at church).

Although we should work if we can, to provide for ourselves and meet our responsibilities, if we find ourselves out of paid employment through no fault of our own, and make every effort to find work and to seek God for a job, then we are fulfilling our responsibility. If we do this with all our heart, get ourselves re-trained if we need to, and if we are prepared to accept available work even if it is not our first choice job, then we can be assured that we have done our part. We need to leave the rest up to God; He will work things out for us. This will require faith, trust and perseverance on a scale that we may never have had to show when work was going well. Remember that the training ground of champions is often the 'wilderness', and in these circumstances it is important to hold on to the biblical truth that '...in all things God works for the good of those who love him, who have been called according to his purpose' (Romans 8:28). God can take us through a time of unemployment to do a new or deeper work in us, or change the course of our life or career. It can be a blessing in disguise.

The experience of unemployment can cause us to withdraw from others and lose confidence. When men meet and talk, they will tend to ask how the job is going. When men meet for the first time they will tend to ask each other what they are doing for a living. If you are unemployed it can be tempting to avoid social contact so that you will not have to answer any awkward questions about work. However, in times of unemployment it is important to maintain social contact. There is also a great need to hold on to the truth that our sense of worth and well-being is rooted in our identity as sons of God. We are still a chosen people, a royal priesthood, a holy nation, a people set apart for Him, whether we have a paid job or not. You do not have to earn that identity—it is a gift of God's grace, and you can hold your head high. As Peter Curran writes: 'Your work is what you do; while it contributes to your self-esteem and character, it does not define your worth. Even if it disappears, you are just as valuable to God.'[1] We can also still work diligently in a way which is pleasing to Him and fulfilling to us, whether we get paid or not. We can still fulfil our calling to be workers should we find ourselves out of paid employment, though it will require courage, perseverance and faith. These are the hallmarks of a champion.

[1] *Op. cit.*, p. 160

SUMMARY OF KEY POINTS

1. Pay is not the defining characteristic of work. Work is about serving through our labour. There are forms of work that can still be glorifying to God and fulfilling to us which attract little or no pay. Such work is not a second class calling.

2. The points raised in the chapter do not negate the importance of being prepared to work for pay, should that be our responsibility and should we be able to do so.

QUESTIONS FOR REFLECTION/DISCUSSION

1. Why do you think 'homemakers' can see their contribution as less valuable than paid work?

2. If you were to write a job advert for the role of 'homemaker', what are some of the points you would include—the difficult aspects and challenges as well as the more enjoyable ones?

3. Read Colossians 3:23. What advice and support do you think you might need to give to a friend who has suddenly lost their job, so that they do not slip into despair?

4. Think about the ways your work influences your self-esteem, and that of your friends and colleagues. In the light of Jeremiah 31:3 and 1 Peter 2:9–10, what should be the source of self esteem for Christians?

5. List the ways in which anything from this chapter or from your review of the above questions applies to you as a working person in your own circumstances. Then list any **actions** you will take as a result of this study (e.g. further study or reflection, prayer, speaking *to someone, requests for help*, changing something about yourself) and be as specific as possible about **when** you will complete the action(s).

13

THE REST IS UP TO YOU

All too often we can feel that we have too much to do and too little time to do it in: too many things to sort out; too much to worry about; too many demands on our time and energy. So much seems to be pressing in and taking more and more out of us. We can feel that we have less and less time to replenish our strength and energy. Our work, our family, our church based activities are all good things, but they demand our time and our mental, emotional and physical energy, as well as our spiritual resources. In the late 1990s, a survey indicated that working lives are getting increasingly out of balance. In the twenty-first century, the picture has certainly not improved. These were some of the key results from the survey:[1]

☐ 84% of the sample admitted that they have made important sacrifices in pursuit of their career—such as missing their children grow up.

☐ Over half claimed that the pressure to perform at work meant less time for a personal life.

---

[1] A survey of about 6000 UK managers was summarised in *Management Today*, June 1998 edition.

☐   About two thirds said that they were expected to ask more and more from the staff working for them, and that long hours tended to get interpreted positively as showing commitment to the company.

Writing about the work and non-work balance in the American context, Kaufman and Quigley[1] have noted that the demands of companies are increasing. They observe that working weeks of sixty hours are the norm. Managers are expected to travel more; email, pagers and mobile phones all mean that workers are on duty for longer. Small wonder, then, that more and more consultancies offer 'work-life balance' courses to help people achieve a balance in their lives so that they do not burn out. When the demands and pressures upon us outweigh our ability to meet the demands, we can feel stressed, and, when stress is sustained, we can become physically or mentally ill. It is worth noting that research indicates that seven of the top thirteen causes of absence from work due to sickness, in the UK, are stress related.

Somehow, we need to keep all aspects of our life in a healthy balance—keeping on top of things; living a victorious life that is free from burn-out and the ill effects of stress.

In a busy life, rest can seem like a luxury, and can too easily get squeezed out of our schedule as having a lower priority than *doing* things. However, neglecting rest will, sooner or later, have an impact upon physical and mental well-being. Neglecting the right kind of rest also has an impact upon spiritual life. Preaching in 1880, D.L. Moody said, 'You show me a nation that has given up the Sabbath and I will show you a nation that has got seeds of decay.' His comment could just as well apply to the spiritual life of individuals and nations today. Moreover, the Bible helps us to understand how we can abide in God and rest in Him *as* we work, thereby releasing us from the burden of worry and frustration that so easily saps our energy. His word even gives us guidance on how to manage our time more effectively—not so that we can do even more, but to teach us how to keep our lives healthy and balanced. Whilst the keys He has given us are simple, the hard part for many of us is to pick them up and use them.

---

[1] *Op. cit.*

KEEP THE SABBATH

God instituted the seventh day as a Sabbath day, or day of rest from work. He rested following the six days of creation:

> By the seventh day God had finished the work he had been doing; so on the seventh day he rested from all his work. And God blessed the seventh day and made it holy, because on it he rested from all the work of creating that he had done.
>
> *Genesis 2:2–3*

God gave us a healthy pattern for living:

> Remember the Sabbath day by keeping it holy. Six days you shall labor and do all your work, but the seventh day is a Sabbath to the Lord your God. On it you shall not do any work, neither you, nor your son or daughter, nor your manservant or maidservant, nor your animals, nor the alien within your gates. For in six days the Lord made the heavens and the earth, the sea, and all that is in them, but he rested on the seventh day. Therefore the Lord blessed the Sabbath day and made it holy.
>
> *Exodus 20:8–11*

The seriousness of God's command on this matter was demonstrated in a remarkable way. For four hundred and ninety years, the people of Israel neglected God's command to let the land have a Sabbath rest every seven years. But they were then taken into exile for seventy years by Nebuchadnezzar, during which time their land was not producing. In effect, the Lord took back all the Sabbath days they had neglected.

God knows best what we need—far better than we do. He knows that we need a break from our work. But the Sabbath is more than that. God knows that we need a particular time set aside to remember Him, to re-focus on Him and to remember the work of salvation, transformation and blessing that He has done in our lives. Of course, our relationship with the Lord, and spending time with Him, is for every day, but the Sabbath provides a whole day for us to be 'repaired' from the previous week and prepared for the week ahead. Taking time to return to Him, and to be renewed and refreshed in Him, helps us keep the pressures of life in healthy perspective and balance. What an excellent preventive approach to stress management! It is important not to be legalistic about this commandment. If someone really has to work on a Sunday, then another day can be the Sabbath rest day; it does not have to be a Sunday. Moreover, in his teaching about the Sabbath, Jesus allowed works of necessity, works of emergency and works of mercy. Activities like these should, however, be exceptions to the general principle that for one day a week we rest and take time to focus on God. Jesus taught us that the Sabbath is made for man.

TAKE REGULAR REST

Peter Curran has defined rest as follows: '...cessation from work—stepping aside from necessary tasks to make space and time for refreshment, recreation, relationships and worship.'[1] Rest is about stopping doing the things that drain us of energy. It is also about starting the things that replenish our energy and strength. Rest is essential to all of us, and Jesus taught the importance of resting when you are tired. When Jesus sent out the twelve to preach, teach, drive out demons and heal, they found themselves very busy. The needs were great around them, and the Lord had given them the authority to meet those needs. They must have felt tremendous responsibility and excitement in their ministry role. They were doing a good job, and had many testimonies to talk about when they returned to Jesus. In a sense, though, they were swamped. People came from all around; they were caught up in their work, and kept busy meeting the endless stream of needs. We can all find ourselves busy to the point of neglecting our own welfare and wellbeing, whether in church based ministry or secular work. Jesus pointed the disciples back to **rest**. It must have felt like a luxury when there was so much to do, but he told them to, "...come with me by yourselves to a quiet place and get some rest"(Mark 6:31.)

[1] *Op. cit.* p. 16

We all need to stop sometimes, when we find ourselves caught up in a busy period of activity. At those times of intense busyness it can feel that taking time out is just impossible. But there will always be more we can do. If we are going to be effective and healthy over the longer-term, we need to make rest a priority in our lifestyle, and particularly in our busy periods. We need to schedule in periods for rest and recuperation. After a busy period of teaching, Jesus took his disciples away from the crowds into a boat. There, we find that, 'Jesus was in the stern, sleeping on a cushion' (Mark 4:38). He practised what he preached.

REST IN CHRIST

It is in our daily personal relationship with God that we will find the strength, encouragement, peace, healing and rest that we need to live out our busy lives. Jesus promises us rest if we *come* to him:

> "Come to me, all you who are weary and burdened, and I will give you rest. Take my yoke upon you and learn from me, for I am gentle and humble in heart, and you will find rest for your souls. For my yoke is easy and my burden is light."
>
> *Matthew 11:28–30*

We need to come to Jesus in repentance and humility, acknowledging that we need his help to get us through. When we choose to walk in God's ways, living in submission to Him, we can be cleansed and released from the burdens that sap our energy and joy, and we can enjoy the rest and freedom that Christ offers us. The rest Jesus speaks about is rest for our soul, which is much deeper than just taking a physical rest for our body. This rest is available to us even as we work, or fulfil our daily activities and responsibilities.

As we learn to trust in God in all areas of our life, and to trust in the truth of the promises in His word, we can enjoy an inner rest in our heart, soul and mind. This will be peace and rest that transcends all situations, pressures, difficulties and crises. It will be a rest that is drawn from our on-going relationship of trust and love with Jesus. There will be strength for us to get through all the things we face when we are quiet before God, stop striving and choose to trust in Him, for, '...in quietness and trust is your strength' (Isaiah 30:15.)

We know from His word that God will provide for us when we put Him first in our life, so why worry and strive? As Jesus said:

> '...do not worry, saying, "what shall we eat?" or "What shall we drink?" or "What shall we wear?" For the pagans run after all these things, and your heavenly Father knows that you need them. But seek first his kingdom and his righteousness, and all these things will be given to you as well.'
>
> *Matthew 6:31–33*

God will provide for our needs when we put Him and His kingdom first. When we grasp the truth of His word that He will always be with us as our ever present help, then we can be still. All striving and worry can stop, and we can be at rest. We may well have a busy work life, but we can still be at rest in the midst of it all when we can accept the Lord's encouragement to:

> 'be still, and know that I am God....'
>
> *Psalm 46:10*

Trusting in God will drive out the fear that robs us of our rest and peace. When the psalmist faced enemies who pursued him, he encouraged himself to trust the Lord:

> When I am afraid, I will trust in you.
> In God, whose word I praise, in God I trust;
> I will not be afraid.
> What can mortal man do to me?
>
> *Psalm 56:3–4*

God wants to help us throughout our lives, and He makes all that we need available to us. But sometimes we need to ask Him for help. He wants us to depend upon Him for help, and He will respond, but He resists the proud and keeps His distance from those who think they can get through purely by their own efforts, talents or strength. We need to approach Him in prayer, and ask Him for help in all circumstances, including those of our work.

> Let us then approach the throne of grace with confidence, so that we may receive mercy and find grace to help us in our time of need.
>
> *Hebrews 4:16*

Why not seek God for His unmerited favour just before a meeting, prior to starting a piece of work, or before a job interview? Throughout the day we can draw upon His help. Short, sharp prayers to Him in the midst of our busyness are a lifeline to His powerful help and favour. Many of us need to become more disciplined about asking, and get ourselves into a position of receiving. We need to bring our relationship with God into the workplace.

Sometimes, things can gnaw away in our thoughts. When we get home, the difficulties, mistakes or struggles of the day can plague the mind. Something that someone has said can erode your peace, and one can spend one's whole evening mulling it over, or talking it through with your spouse. When you put your head on the pillow, it can all come flooding back, and it seems impossible to forget about it. You can then be robbed of rest, perhaps even waking during the night with the same thoughts. We can, of course, pray and ask for God's help. Paul teaches us to do this:

> Do not be anxious about anything, but in everything, by prayer and petition, with thanksgiving, present your requests to God. And the peace of God, which transcends all understanding, will guard your hearts and your minds in Christ Jesus.
>
> *Philippians 4:6–7*

Prayer is a key to rest, and, besides praying for ourselves, we can also ask someone else to pray for us on a regular basis or when we are particularly troubled. If the source of our anxiety or disquiet is that someone else has wronged us in some way, actively forgiving that person and asking God to forgive and bless them can also be a powerful way to be released from our troubled thoughts. If we forgive the person, there can no longer be a dispute going on in our mind. There is no longer a need to rehearse our case against them, nor to dwell on the injustice we feel. The matter has been sorted out.

Paul gave the Philippians another key to ensuring a healthy life—simply, choose to think about good things. During the day, and as we reflect on the events of our working day in the evening, there will be many negative things that our thoughts can dwell on: the people, the work, the injustice, the unfairness, the boredom, the frustration, the lies, the backbiting. The list can go on. However, Paul urges us to get a grip on our thoughts, and choose to fill our mind with thoughts about good things, thinking positively rather than negatively:

> Finally, brothers, whatever is true, whatever is noble, whatever is right, whatever is pure, whatever is lovely, whatever is admirable —if anything is excellent or praiseworthy—think about such things.
>
> *Philippians 4:8*

God fulfils all these criteria, of course, and we can think about Him instead of some foolish thing our colleague said to us or about us. We can start by cultivating the habit of short prayers and brief moments of worship during our work. Ask your heavenly Father to help you. Thank Him for His help. Tell Him you love Him. It only takes a moment.

MANAGE YOUR TIME

We are called to be *good stewards* of our time. We are called to be consistently productive, effective and fruitful in the things that count, and to make best use of our God-given talents. However, we are not called to be overloaded and stressed—focussing on things of minor significance, to the exclusion of the more important ones. Neither are we called to spread ourselves across so many activities that we are not effective at anything. Most of us have too much to do, and too little time. We therefore need to ensure that we use the resource of time wisely. Here are some tips for how to manage your time.

BE CLEAR ON THE OVERALL PURPOSE FOR YOUR LIFE AND YOUR CHOSEN LIFESTYLE

Being clear on what matters most to you in life, and where you are aiming for, is an important first step towards effective time management. God has clear plans behind what He does. In Jeremiah 29:11, He said, 'For I know the plans I have for you...'

and in Lamentations we read that, 'The LORD has done what he planned; he has fulfilled his word, which he decreed long ago...' (2:17). Similarly, being clear about how work commitments and ambitions fit into your overall lifestyle and longer-term plans and goals is important. If I am clear, for example, that I want a healthy family as well as success in my work, then I will ensure that weekends (or equivalent blocks of time off) are for my family and church. I will manage my work schedule quite differently than I would were success in my career to be my only long-term goal. Otherwise, I might see the weekend as a time when I can finish things off that I do not manage to complete at work, or as an opportunity to demonstrate greater commitment than my colleagues (and the family would have to understand). It is important to remember that spending time on some things will mean less time for other things, and that ultimately we all have choices to make. Unless we first make the choices about what is ultimately important for us, and then manage our activities accordingly, the circumstances and external demands on our time will tend to make the choices for us.

SET THE BROAD PRIORITIES

Once you know where you are heading in life and what matters to you, then be clear about allocating your time. What are your top three priorities or goals for the year ahead? This exercise can be done in relation to both work-related activities and non-work related aspects of life. Setting priorities is a biblical principle. We learn from Proverbs that it is best to sort out the most important and fundamental things first, then concentrate on the detail:

> Finish your outdoor work and get your fields ready; after that, build your house.
>
> *Proverbs 24:27*

Take some time to reflect on the extent to which the use of your time is consistent with what matters most to you. What are some of the practical steps you could take to get your use of time clearly in line with the lifestyle you aim for, and your main goals and priorities?

COMMIT YOUR TIME TO THE LORD

Our time is a gift from God, and we are stewards of it. There is peace, release and assurance when we give it back to Him on a daily basis, ask Him to work out His plan and purpose in our day and help us in all we do. When we are pressurised and focused on a particular problem or task, it can be all too easy to forget this principle.

> Commit to the Lord whatever you do, and your plans will succeed.
> *Proverbs 16:3*

BE CLEAR ABOUT WHAT YOU NEED TO DO

Now list all the tasks that you need to do. Your list may cover the immediate day ahead but also include things that need action in the week or month ahead. You will need to keep this list up to date, revising it as new tasks are given to you. Tasks or activities can be crossed off when completed.

PRIORITISE YOUR ACTIVITIES

The next step is to assess the relative importance of the 'things to do'. This can be done by evaluating the *urgency* and *importance* of each activity in the context of the requirements of your job. The same approach can, of course, be used for non-work activities or commitments. The list below illustrates the general principle: this can help us decide what tasks to do now or later, and which tasks not to do at all. The story of Martha and Mary (Luke 10:38–42) illustrates the crucial difference between *urgency* and *importance*. Martha busied herself with the *urgent* domestic preparations for Jesus' visit. Mary busied herself with the *important* activity of sitting at the Lord's feet, and he commended her, saying she, 'has chosen what is better.' Whatever is urgent may not be what is most important, and ultimately it is doing the important things that matters.

Important, but not so urgent
Schedule to do it later, but make sure it gets done.

Important and urgent
Must be done as soon as possible.

Not so important and not so urgent
Do not do it or agree to do it. If these tasks have to be done, consider delegating them.

Urgent, but not so important
Get some or all of these tasks out of the way quickly, but do not spend too much time. Consider delegating these tasks.

PLAN YOUR DAY, BUT BE FLEXIBLE

Once you have prioritised the tasks, decide which ones must be tackled today. Estimate as *realistically* as possible, how long each of these tasks will take, and book in a time slot to your schedule for the day to deal with each of them. You should also allow time to deal with any unexpected matters that may arise. Remember how God allocated one main specific act of creation—or objective—to each of the first six days (Genesis 1:6–8). We need to pace ourselves, and to do what we need to in 'chunks' that are meaningful, and which, realistically, can be fitted in to the day. Once you have a plan for a specific day, it is good to check how well the plan fits with the broad life priorities and commitments you identified originally. If, for example, one of your broad priorities is to build a network of friends or contacts, how well is that reflected in your plan for the day or week ahead?

While we can plan the day, it is also important to be flexible. Sometimes, our plans will have to change, and we will have to deal with unexpected things. However, this does not make planning a waste of time. In fact, it may be even more important to plan, so that we keep track of those things that we cannot afford to lose sight of. Many people will also say that there is no time to prioritise and plan: 'I haven't got time to plan, I've just got too much to do, and I need to get on with it.' However, cultivating a planned approach to daily life will both help reduce time wasted on activities of low urgency and importance and will help minimise the sense of pressure when we feel that we are swamped. Planning may seem difficult and may feel like a luxury at first, but it will prove a good investment of time.

PLAN—DO—REVIEW; AND BACK AGAIN

Spending a few minutes reviewing the day can be time well spent. It will help to identify what has been achieved and what needs to be carried forward to the next day. Reviewing can also help identify how your planning and time management can be further improved, such as by estimating more accurately how long activities will take to complete, or becoming more aware of the things that have wasted your time. Remember how God reviewed His creation work at the end of each day—saw that it was good, and took pleasure in what He had done (Genesis 1:4, 10, 12 & 31).

SOMETIMES YOU HAVE TO SAY 'NO' —IN THE NICEST POSSIBLE WAY

When you look closely at what you do, you can often find that you are busy because you are doing unnecessary things, or doing things inefficiently. A good worker, or a co-operative person, is often presented with more work to do because others trust them to get things done. While saying 'yes' to more can win us some short-term popularity, in the long term—if we persistently take on too much, or waste time on less important things—we will suffer, and the quality of our work will also suffer. Sometimes, we will have to say 'no' to ensure our activities fit with our overall purpose and priorities in life and with the key purpose of our job.

Saying 'no' at work can be difficult, and will often require a careful explanation in the context of a co-operative working relationship ('I can't do it now because I have to do various other things, but I will be able to do it by....') Cutting out certain activities that add little or no value may also be necessary—such as attendance at unproductive meetings, unnecessary tasks that may have always been done but are really pointless. Delegation of work helps to ensure that you are not consistently overloaded. Peter Curran has given a useful example of how to say 'no' to a request to work late: 'A straightforward way of saying "no" would be: "No I'm sorry. I know you have a problem in getting someone, but I am unable to help tonight".' Whilst this is clear and to the point, it is not offensive. If you are a conscientious worker, with a right attitude and a good relationship with the boss, then occasionally saying 'no' should not be a problem, as long as it is legitimate to do so.

SOME PRACTICAL TIPS

Some suggestions follow as to how we can get our life in balance and build in adequate rest time. Some of them may seem obvious, but, sometimes, when we are too busy we can lose sight of the obvious. Can you add any further suggestions to the list?

☐ Stop doing unnecessary things.
☐ Prioritise your responsibilities and commitments and stop doing the low priority or less urgent ones—do them later or not at all.
☐ Schedule your annual leave ahead of time rather than waiting for a good time to take it—a good time to take leave may never come! If possible, manage workload and responsibilities around your leave rather than the other way around.
☐ Take the occasional Friday or Monday off, to make a long weekend.
☐ Take exercise, rather than inactive leisure such as just sleeping or watching television.
☐ Spend time with the Lord and His word in the morning and the evening—this can give us a healthy focus. We can ask Him to help, cleanse and strengthen us. Just enjoy His presence.
☐ Spend time in worship and prayer during the day. Ask for God's help when you face a task, and thank Him for His help when it has been completed.

☐ If you have been really busy, schedule some recovery time, rather than just going straight on to the next task.

☐ Try to get jobs done on Saturday rather than on Sunday (if Sunday is your Sabbath).

☐ Train to make yourself more effective in your job. Read the Bible (e.g. Proverbs, the life of Daniel and Joseph) to understand how you can be more effective in your work.

☐ Where possible and appropriate, delegate work. Delegation should not be dumping on others the tasks you do not want, it should help develop other people, and assist in achieving greater productivity.

☐ Re-negotiate your workload with your boss if you consistently have too much to do.

☐ Be clear about your limits—such as how much overtime you are prepared to work, and, where possible, learn to say 'no' if you are pressured to work beyond your limits.

☐ Forgive those who may be working against you or competing with you. Strife drains away your energy and sense of peace. Take practical steps to demonstrate that forgiveness.

☐ Develop a hobby or interest outside your work.

☐ Place a priority on fellowship with other Christians.

SUMMARY OF KEY POINTS

1. One important facet of our God-given pattern of life is rest from work. He makes provision for rest times, such as the Sabbath.

2. A profoundly important aspect of our life in Christ is learning to rest in Him daily —by trusting and abiding in Him.

3. There are many simple and practical steps we can take to build rest and balance into a healthy lifestyle, managing our time more effectively.

4. Rest is under attack. Therefore, you may need to re-discover rest, or take steps to build it back into your life.

TIME TO ASK YOURSELF SOME QUESTIONS

Having considered some aspects of work and rest, you may find it useful to complete the questionnaire which follows. The questions are designed to aid self-reflection and to help you begin to identify specific areas where personal change and development are needed. First, complete all the ratings in the 'Self Assessment' column; then reflect on which aspects of time management you need to improve on, by completing all the ratings in the 'Priority for Improvement' column ('Low', 'Medium' or 'High' priority for improvement). You will not be able to improve everything at once, so pick out the few aspects that are likely to have most benefit, and concentrate on improving those things first. Over time, come back to your responses to the questionnaire and identify further things to improve.

You could also use the questionnaire and your responses as the basis for a group discussion. Other people may have some useful tips, and you could also make suggestions that could help someone else.

ASPECT OF TIME MANAGEMENT	Self Assessment 1= Never 2 = Seldom 3 = Often 4 = Always	Priority for Improvement
Clear Priorities and Objectives		
I am clear what my priorities in life are.	1 2 3 4	Low Med High
I am committed to doing too many things in life.	1 2 3 4	Low Med High
I prioritise the things I have to do, focusing upon the important things rather than just the urgent things.	1 2 3 4	Low Med High
I have a clear job description and I know what I should be doing at work.	1 2 3 4	Low Med High
I have clear short term and long term objectives that are simple, measurable, achievable, realistic and have clear deadlines/ timescales.	1 2 3 4	Low Med High
I do the things that need doing, not just the things that I like doing most.	1 2 3 4	Low Med High
I keep my attention focused on the things that matter.	1 2 3 4	Low Med High
I can and do say 'no' to taking on more tasks when I need to.	1 2 3 4	Low Med High
I find myself spending time doing completely unnecessary things.	1 2 3 4	Low Med High
I deal with priority tasks at the start of the day or at the right time.	1 2 3 4	Low Med High

Planning		
I plan my day, allowing time for reactive tasks, and booking in slots where I can get on with the work that can be planned ahead.	1 2 3 4	Low Med High
I plan ahead, but I am realistic about how long unplanned things will take.	1 2 3 4	Low Med High
I make realistic assessments of how long planned things will take to get done.	1 2 3 4	Low Med High
I keep a diary of planned events, meetings, activities, etc.	1 2 3 4	Low Med High
I keep a written daily schedule/ planner of all the things I need to do.	1 2 3 4	Low Med High
There are no parts of my job that take more time than they should.	1 2 3 4	Low Med High
Basic Controls		
I control my time rather than just react to things as they happen.	1 2 3 4	Low Med High
I do not waste time.	1 2 3 4	Low Med High
I have a tidy desk with everything in an appropriate place.	1 2 3 4	Low Med High
I use a tidy and well organised filing system.	1 2 3 4	Low Med High
I delegate tasks appropriately to others and monitor their progress.	1 2 3 4	Low Med High

I attend meetings on time.	1 2 3 4	Low Med High
I forget about some meetings or appointments, or double book myself.	1 2 3 4	Low Med High
I keep my meetings and telephone conversations to the point.	1 2 3 4	Low Med High
I take rest and meal breaks during my day.	1 2 3 4	Low Med High
I deal with paperwork straight away, and only deal with it once.	1 2 3 4	Low Med High
I finish the things that I start.	1 2 3 4	Low Med High
I get things done on time and within budget.	1 2 3 4	Low Med High
I keep track of activities that are ongoing.	1 2 3 4	Low Med High
Rest		
I keep a Sabbath day free from work, and spend time with the Lord.	1 2 3 4	Low Med High
I organise my time so that I spend quality time with my family and/ or friends.	1 2 3 4	Low Med High
I spend time in fellowship with other Christians.	1 2 3 4	Low Med High
I spend quality time with the Lord on a daily basis.	1 2 3 4	Low Med High
I plan and book in my leave ahead of time rather than waiting for a good time to take it.	1 2 3 4	Low Med High

I wake up at night worrying about work.	1 2 3 4	Low Med High
I spend my leisure time in a way that is refreshing.	1 2 3 4	Low Med High

The Lord's help		
I daily commit my time and my day to the Lord, no matter how busy I am.	1 2 3 4	Low Med High
I ask the Lord to help me at different times during the day.	1 2 3 4	Low Med High
I can get the things of the day out of my mind when I leave work, and ask the Lord to help me do so.	1 2 3 4	Low Med High

In terms of interpreting your ratings, you will need to take stock of your strengths and opportunities for development. Firstly, try to describe the general pattern of results. For example, are you generally weakest in terms of the items under one or some of the headings in the questionnaire—such as a lack of basic controls; or are there a few specific items under all of the headings where you may need to improve? Secondly, you will need to decide which issues to try to tackle first. You will not be able to tackle everything at once, but try to identify those aspects of time management where it is most important that you improve (lowest self assessment and highest priority to improve). These will generally be the specific aspects of time management that have most impact on your life now. ('If only I got that right, things would be a lot better.') You can re-visit your ratings and review your progress regularly. Try doing the questionnaire again in six months, and see if the profile of ratings is any different.

NEXT STEPS

List any **actions** you intend to take as a result of this study (e.g. further study or reflection, prayer, speaking to someone, requests for help, changing something about yourself) and be as specific as possible about **when** you will complete the action(s).

14

MONEY, MONEY, MONEY

For those of us working outside the home, money will be the main reward for our work. Money, as such, is not an evil: it pays for the things we need. It is essential if we are going to support those who depend on us. It also means that we can have some of the enjoyable things of life, such as a holiday, and it gives us the opportunity to be generous to others, and to support the work of the kingdom of God, and causes that are important to us.

But money can also be the root cause of a lot of problems, tragedy and heartache. Nowadays, we can get into debt almost effortlessly, and living beyond our means can be the root cause of much misery and grief. The burden of debt can fuel conflict in relationships and can lead to the breakdown of marriages and family relationships. Loans and credit are only a phone call or an e-mail away. If we are earning, then retailers make it easy for us to arrange purchases on credit, and we are an attractive target for them. Brochures from credit card companies flow through our letterboxes, offering attractive deals. We are bombarded by images of what we could have, and arranging credit is such a tempting way to get all the things we want—now, rather than by waiting. The misleading message is clear: 'You can have all that you want now, and pay later on. You do not need to live within your means and wait until you have earned enough to afford the things you want.' The money we have can multiply our debt. It has been pointed out that many people drive a car bought with a loan, to do shopping paid for by a credit card, to take back to a house which is mortgaged. Borrowing to pay off debts just makes the situation worse. It is a slippery slope that is hard to get off.

The love of money—or the love of what money can buy—can be a snare. Some people at work are constantly disgruntled about money ('why should he earn more than me...what a miserable pay rise, it's an insult....') Some define 'success' in terms of money, and their self esteem and sense of worth can be tied up in how much they earn and what possessions they have. As a result, they will never be satisfied, because there will always be someone else who earns more than they do.

It is important for us to have a godly approach to managing money. Money needs to be our servant and not our master.

GOOD STEWARDS

Being a good steward of the money we earn is key to maintaining a life that is free from the bondage of debt and the burden of poverty; and it is key to enjoying the blessing of God in our life. There is an eternal perspective in all this. If we are to lay up treasures in heaven rather than just here on earth, we need to manage the finances we have now and do so in God's way. We need to be good stewards. The word 'steward' in the Greek is 'oikonomia', meaning 'administration; managing as an estate'. As stewards we have the responsibility and privilege of looking after God's estate for Him.

Our starting point needs to be that the money we earn belongs to God—even though we have earned it through our labour. We are just looking after it for Him, and He has given us some guiding principles for how to manage it on His behalf. The money which we earn and that appears on our bank statements is 'ours', but in reality everything is *God's*. As we follow His principles, we will enjoy many blessings. Instead of multiplying debt, burden and trouble, managing money in God's way will multiply the benefit and blessing; it is His way which will keep us free from the burden of debt or poverty. So what are His principles for good stewardship?

Firstly, God promises to provide for us, protect what we have and bless us when we honour Him by giving a tenth of what we earn to the storehouse, which we should take to be our church. Tithing is not a principle invented by churches to make money. Tithing is a means by which we acknowledge that God has provided for us, and we choose to willingly give Him back part of what he has already given to us. By giving back to God what is His anyway, we express our thanks, trust, faith and dependence on Him. When we honour God, He will honour us, and He promises that He will bless us when we tithe. It is the only place in the Bible where God challenges us to test Him:

> "Bring the whole tithe into the storehouse, that there may be food in my house. Test me in this," says the Lord Almighty, "and see if I will not throw open the floodgates of heaven and pour out so much blessing that you will not have room enough for it."
>
> *Malachi 3:10*

Regular weekly or monthly tithing on our gross earnings is a good pattern to get into. At first, it can feel as though we are giving away a big chunk of our money. That can be a bit painful, particularly if we are not sure how our hard-earned money will be used. It can be awkward if our fellowship does not encourage tithing. The principle of tithing can rub against the grain of our church tradition, but it is for each of us to prayerfully reflect upon our position regarding giving.

What a comfort it is, when we hit difficult times, to know that we have been faithful in honouring God in our giving. We can be assured that He will provide for us. I once lost my job with a consultancy firm. The company was not making enough money, and as I was the last in so I was the first one out. During that period in between jobs, money came in, and as a family we had more money than we had ever had when I was working! My wife and I have always been faithful in tithing, and when we needed God's help, He provided for us. People who did not know our predicament wrote enclosing money gifts. We had plenty, and through the experience of job loss, God opened up a new career path that has proved to be much more fulfilling and financially rewarding. God is true to His word.

Secondly, we should live within our means. We read in Proverbs that:

> The rich rule over the poor,
> and the borrower is servant to the lender.
>
> *Proverbs 22:7*

In other words, when we borrow money through loans or credit, we give the lender power over us. We relinquish something of our freedom. We lose some of the control over our lives, and the ability to decide what to do with the resources that God has entrusted to us. Of course, most of us have to borrow from a lender to buy our family home. However, there is a crucial difference between prudent and careful borrowing for essentials such as a house, and extravagant and unnecessary borrowing that enslaves us and puts a burden upon our back that is hard to bear. We need to live within our means. If that entails having to wait a few years for the nice furniture and the new car, then it may be better to live with what we have than start to accumulate debt.

We may need to exercise self-control. If you see something that you think you need and want to buy, leave it for a while. It may be that, after a few days, it no longer seems such a necessity. It may begin to look more like something you *want* rather than something you *need*. Living within our means also necessitates some form of basic financial planning and monitoring. We need to budget our expenditure (e.g. accommodation, food, bills, clothing, transport) based on what is coming in as income, and we need to monitor our expenditure against the budget so that we keep our finances under control. A simple step to take is to keep a record of all you spend so that you do not lose track of how much you have left to cover purchases or expenditure for that week or month. For many of us, this will require taking some time to review our finances on a regular basis, asking some basic questions like these:

☐ Exactly how much income do I have this week/ month?
☐ What bills/expenses will I have to pay this week/month?
☐ How much do I tend to spend this time of year as unplanned expenses?
☐ How much will I have to save to pay for things next month or in the near future, or for contingencies?

☐ How much do I have left after taking the expenditure and savings from the income?

Here are some useful and basic tips for how to live within your means, and how to get things under control if you have got into budgeting difficulties.

Cut your spending:

☐ Resist the pressure of advertising.
☐ Look out for the best buy.
☐ Shop for necessities in the sales.
☐ Stop dining out in restaurants.
☐ Restrict and carefully control your use of credit cards.
☐ Do not use future income to meet current requirements.
☐ Consider whether something you wish to buy is really a need.

Set up a method of control by:

☐ Preparing a budget—include your income, savings, tithes, offerings, expenditure;
☐ Reviewing income and expenditure regularly;
☐ Basing decisions and judgements on the Lord's ways by:
☐ practising the precepts in His word, including being honest and upright in all dealings; establishing a continuing programme of tithing, giving;
☐ Observing biblical principles of stewardship;
☐ Seeking Christian counsel.

Re-evaluate your lifestyle:

☐ How do you eat or dress?
☐ How much do you spend on cars?
☐ Ask yourself whether you are wasteful.
☐ Make prudent savings (not hoarding).
☐ Improve your skills, and consider getting a better job.

Thirdly, if we give generously to the work of God's kingdom and to the needy, we will reap generously in return. This was a principle Paul tried to teach the Corinthian church:

> Remember this: Whoever sows sparingly will also reap sparingly, and whoever sows generously will also reap generously. Each man should give what he has decided in his heart to give, and not reluctantly or under compulsion, for God loves a cheerful giver.
>
> *2 Corinthians 9:6–7*

Stewardship has helpfully been defined as: '...a life commitment to real care for one another, to living generously and to practical care for our environment' (Keith Tondeur). At the heart of it is generosity, giving to benefit others in a way that involves personal sacrifice. It involves giving more than the bare minimum—more than the tithe. There are many ways in which we can live generously, and causes that we can give to. We can support our local church over and above our tithe. Our tithe is the minimum; it is what we already owe God, and we only really start giving when we give more than that. We can support Christians in church based ministry including those who have taught us God's word, mission workers and other programmes, as well as fellow Christians who are in need. The poor have a special place in God's heart, and there will always be relatively poor people around us. God has given us responsibility to meet the needs of the poor.

> If a man shuts his ears to the cry of the poor,
> he too will cry out and not be answered.
>
> *Proverbs 21:13*

There are many needs, endless needs, but when we give with a good motive, it is pleasing to God, and He will trust us with more. The key to financial freedom, rather than financial bondage, is giving. God has led us by His own example to a life of giving. He gave Himself in Jesus for our benefit. Giving is at the heart of our Christian witness. We are called to give generously but wisely, and to be hospitable. When we can give freely to others—from the resources God has entrusted to us— then we know that we have been released from bondage to money.

The fourth key principle of good stewardship is to put God first in our life. He promises that, when we do so, He will take care of all our material needs:

> But seek first his kingdom and his righteousness, and all these things will be given to you as well.
>
> *Matthew 6:33*

The 'things' Jesus was referring to included the necessities of life, such as food, drink and clothing. We need to be careful to go on putting God first, even when our earnings increase and we have more than just the necessities of life. By doing so, we will ensure there will be no room for money and material things to become a snare, a source of pride, a stumbling block or idols in our lives. He will take care of our needs.

The focus of our hearts must not be on the wealth we have but on the Giver, and we need to be clear about Who has provided the wealth in the first place. Our perspective needs to be an eternal one, and our real concern is to be with laying up treasure in heaven, rather than striving for more wealth in this life. It is good to have plenty, but not if it dulls our zeal and love for God, nor if we lose sight of the fact that we depend on Him for everything, and that everything we have belongs to Him.

There should be no reason to constantly strive for more money in a way that takes away our peace of mind. We should learn to be content at all times—like Paul. God is our paymaster, and if we live and work according to His principles and standards, then we can be assured that He will meet our needs. He will bless and reward our work and prosper us in His time. Of course there may be periods in life when things are relatively tight financially, but through our work we serve and honour the Lord who promises that He will supply all our needs, according to His riches.

MORE PAY?

There will be times in our lives when we will need more money, and hence more pay. When children come along, our expenses will increase. More money is needed when the children go to school or university. Life can get more expensive for a whole variety of reasons. Following the principles of good stewardship will ensure that we make the best use of our income. Also, as we put God first in our life and give generously to the work of His kingdom, and meet the needs of others, we can live in the patient and confident expectation of His provision for our needs. The Philippians were generous towards Paul when he was in need. He thanked them for their generosity, and referred to their financial gifts as 'a fragrant offering, an acceptable sacrifice, pleasing to God' (Philippians 4:18). As they were givers first, Paul assured them that God would supply for them: 'And my God will meet all your needs according to his glorious riches in Christ Jesus' (Philippians 4:19). When we make God the Lord of our finances, and live generously, it is good to know that He will always take care of our needs. But we must be good stewards and givers first. If we have a need, then we can ask God, in prayer, to provide more money. However, the motive behind our asking is all-important. Asking for more in order to meet genuine needs and to be a channel of blessing to others is likely to meet with God's favour. Asking for more in order to accumulate the trappings of wealth and to live an extravagant lifestyle, to please the flesh, is another matter. All kinds of problems and troubles can follow from such a motive, as Paul wrote:

> People who want to get rich fall into temptation and a trap and into many foolish and harmful desires that plunge men into ruin and destruction.
>
> *1 Timothy 6:9*

It is vital to honour God in the work we do and in the way we do it. When we honour Him, He will bless us. Reflecting upon his career and his five promotions in six years, Don Latham writes: 'Our part is to honour Him by giving our best and doing our work to please Him. If you seek to excel in your work, to give your best, to be creative, and are open to new ways of working and you are enthusiastic, it tends to lead to promotion—providing personal satisfaction and challenge'.

You can also take many practical steps to help increase the value of your labour to your employer. You could, for example:

☐ Improve your skills, learn new ones and make sure that your knowledge and skills are up to date. You can do this through attending training courses, reading relevant material, asking questions, taking the initiative to find things out, and being proactive in practising new ways of working. Taking on a project which is slightly different from your normal day to day work can also help extend your skills and contacts in the organisation where you work.

☐ Ask your employer for a higher rate of pay if there is a legitimate case. There may be a company process for applying for a pay review. If not, identify the best way of making and presenting your case for a pay rise to your employer.

☐ Look for another job while prayerfully asking God to show you His will regarding your job. Ask Him to open the right door and close all others as you seek His will. He may, of course, want you to stay where you are with your current employer, and choose to bless you there in His time. It may be important, however, to get used to the idea of changing employer or job. One Christian I know worked for the same company for a long time, thinking that it was better to show loyalty to his employer than to put the needs of his family first. It certainly is good to be a loyal employee, but he suddenly realised that his responsibility should also be to his family and to meeting their needs. As a result he got a better paid job with a new employer, though leaving had been a difficult step as he was comfortable where he was.

☐ Pray for God to give you wisdom and creativity, so that you can do a better job and be 'worth' more to your employer. Solomon asked for wisdom, and God gave it to him.

☐ Be more creative in the way you work. Identify improvements or savings that will benefit your employer, and make sure he/she hears about them before someone else claims the credit! Ask God to give you creativity and make you more productive.

☐ If you change job and employer, negotiate for a starting salary that is realistic but as high as possible and comparable with that of others already in the company doing the same job. Remember, employers should not base their pay offer on the pay that your current employer gives—but on what is appropriate for the job they are employing you to do.

☐ Claim the promise of Malachi 3:10–12 in prayer, and wait patiently for God's answer through whatever door He opens. He will provide for your needs and bless you in His time and in His way.

☐ Seek career counselling or guidance to explore your job/career options and identify what steps you need to take, such as further training, or gaining specific experience, to achieve your preferred option(s).

☐ Ask for feedback from your manager about the things you do well and how you can improve your performance and prepare yourself for a higher level role or promotion. Good feedback can show you some specific things you can work on to improve. Most managers do not like giving feedback, so you may need to ask.

It is important to remember that God blesses, out of His abundant grace—and not because we have earned it. It does not necessarily indicate that we are living an unrighteous life if we do not see a financial blessing. Similarly, a financial increase does not necessarily mean that a person is living a righteous life that is pleasing to Him. We can follow the principles of good stewardship and take practical steps to increase our earning potential. The rest is up to God.

SUMMARY OF KEY POINTS

1. God wants us to be good stewards of the material blessings that He entrusts to us, and the Bible lays down some clear principles of good stewardship for us to follow.

2. There are many practical steps that we can take to increase our earning potential, such as improving our skills and work performance. As Christians we cannot afford to fall behind in our skills compared to others—we should be the most diligent workers!

3. Ultimately, we need to make the Lord our paymaster and live our whole lives in a way which is pleasing to Him and which glorifies Him. We need to commit our ways and our needs to Him, and live in faith that He will provide for us according to His *glorious riches*. Our focus should not be on accumulating riches on earth, but upon using the resources that He has entrusted to us for His kingdom.

QUESTIONS FOR REFLECTION/DISCUSSION

1. Read Proverbs 22:7. What are some of the pressures or temptations to get into significant debt that people face nowadays?

2. What advice regarding money management would you give to a young friend who is just starting a first paid job?

3. What practical steps can people take to ensure they do not get into financial difficulties?

4. In the light of the following verses, what do you think the Christian approach to saving money should be? Proverbs 13:22; Matthew 6:19–21

5. Read Malachi 3:8–12 and 2 Corinthians 9:7. What place do you think tithing has in the life of Christians?

6. What are some of the practical steps that you could take to increase your earning potential?

7. Do you think that Christians should be the richest people on earth?

8. List the ways in which anything from this chapter or from your review of the above questions applies to you as a working person in your own circumstances. Then list any **actions** you will take as a result of this study (e.g. further study or reflection, prayer, speaking to someone, requests for help, changing something about yourself) and be as specific as possible about **when** you will complete the action(s).

15

WITNESS WHILE YOU WORK

Our workplace is just as much a 'mission field' as any foreign nation or unreached people group. In our workplace we will probably work with atheists, agnostics, Hindus, Muslims, even some satanists, 'new agers' and pagans. There may be freemasons in positions of power and influence. There are likely to be hurt people who would never dream of setting foot in a church to find help or guidance, and who think church is all about robes, religious rituals and rules. There may be backslidden Christians who have been disappointed or hurt by other Christians at some time in their life, or who have fallen back into a life of sin. There will be people whose work, success, power or wealth is their 'god', and people who think that Christians are weak-minded fools who cannot face up to the tough reality of a meaningless existence. We will find all sorts at work. We will come face to face with people who have never heard the good news of Jesus Christ; and we might be the only Christian they know. We will work alongside those we would really rather avoid, and we will be with them for anything up to about sixty to seventy per cent of our waking lives. We will live 'cheek by jowl' with people whose values and perspective on life, God and death are completely alien to ours— people who need to know God; people who will test our faith and even oppose us because of our faith. We will set foot in places where the devil has had a grip on peoples' lives and where he has had too much influence over the way things are done. Our workplace is, therefore, a microcosm of a non-Christian world: a real mission field.

For many of us, church is the focus for support of mission fields and the setting which we generally associate with programmes for reaching out to needy people. But what an opportunity God has placed before us. What potential there is for God to use us to reach our colleagues. As working people, we are uniquely placed to get to know non-Christians, make friends with them and have an impact on their lives by pointing them to Jesus. We do not need to go searching them out, or knocking on the doors of complete strangers—they are right there with us, everyday. 'By bringing his love and principles into the working world through the quality of our work, our character and our witness, we are his ambassadors in the most accessible mission field there is.' (Peter Curran) We need to begin to grasp the reality of this unique opportunity and the responsibility, even honour, that God has placed into our hands to represent Him there. As God's champions in the workplace, we first of all need to see ourselves as missionaries, wherever we are: ambassadors for Christ; people through whom God can extend His kingdom, and whom He can use to save souls and to touch lives. We have just as much responsibility to be witnesses to the lost as any missionary on foreign soil. What an honour to work among the heathen, to represent the King of Kings. Even if it does not always feel like an honour, nonetheless it is.

Once we see ourselves as missionaries for Christ in our workplace mission field, we need to live it out in our practical day to day reality, and on a moment by moment basis, in all our actions and words. In a nutshell, being a witness in the workplace is about how much we manifest Jesus, who is in us, to others through the sort of people we are, by how we work, through what we say and how we behave. If there is something genuinely different, or unique, about us as Christians, then it will show, and people will detect it. This will be true of our weaknesses as well as the good things about us. A right relationship with the Lord, and a heart that has been touched and transformed by Him, are therefore essential if we are to be effective witnesses for Him. If we really know God and He is living in us, then, when people probe and test what we are really like, they will find something good there—it will be real. Then, working from the inside outwards, if Christ in us is going to impact others through us, we need to connect with people through friendships, and good quality working relationships. We need to be a part of peoples' lives and let others be a part of our lives. We need to be real people who have a positive impact on others as we get to know them. A smile, a compliment, a 'thank you' for work well done, a simple act of kindness or a word of encouragement, can go a long way when they are weighed down with worries, and when they feel frustrated or unappreciated. In the context of good relationships, the kind of things we say and do can certainly point people to Jesus. Mark Greene has put it succinctly: '...witnessing to Him is living that message in our human flesh. It is being and doing and speaking... living the gospel in such a way that the difference it makes is communicated non-verbally.'[1]

We can draw people to Jesus or point them to him by who we are, by working to a godly standard of excellence and by being 'salt' and 'light' in the context of good working relationships and friendships. This will provide the most meaningful context for sharing the good news of Jesus Christ more directly, should the opportunity arise. However, if we try to share the gospel without the context of a good working relationship, and a positive witness through who we are and how we work, then people can feel threatened or suspicious, and our words may have little credibility. We may not lead to the Lord everyone with whom we make friends at work, but our witness may be one of a number of positive influences and a stepping stone in His plan to draw them to Himself. We might not see the immediate fruit ourselves in terms of people committing their lives to God—it may take a long time to see any results—but He will take care of that in His time and in His way. We are all learning! It is not easy to be a witness at work, and none of us is perfect. We may make mistakes or misjudge people and situations. Thankfully, however, God is patient and merciful, and will help us. Thankfully, too, it is He who does the saving! While we need to be effective and sensitive

---

[1] In *Thank God it's Monday: Ministry in the Workplace*, Scripture Union, 1997

witnesses, it is God at work in peoples' lives Who will bring them to Him. He has a plan for our colleagues, and our role is to point them to Him through our witness. Thankfully, too, being a witness is about being ourselves; it is not an artificial process, programme or set formula. It is about real people like you and me showing the reality of Jesus in the reality of our daily lives.

A HEART AND VISION FOR WORKPLACE MISSIONS

How much do we really care about the eternal destiny of our colleagues? Does the issue of their souls ever occur to us, or is that something for someone else to be concerned about—such as those in full time ministry at church? How much do we want our workplace to be our mission field? It is worth giving an honest answer to these questions. It is good to spend a moment reflecting on what is in your heart, because to be a witness in the workplace you need a heart for God and a heart for the lost. We need to have received the love of God; to have experienced the reality of His care, grace, kindness and faithfulness in our lives. What is required is a heart that loves God out of a realisation of what He has done for you, even though you have not deserved it; and so much so that you want others to know Him and have the same blessing of knowing Him that you, yourself, have experienced. Only when our actions flow from a heart that is transformed by the Holy Spirit will we bear the fruit that He alone can grow in us. When we appreciate the grace we have received from God, we can then learn to express that grace to others in practical ways: it flows out, through us, to others. When we have experienced His forgiveness, we can more readily forgive our colleagues when they harm us and we can express the reality of forgiveness by how we choose to maintain good working relationships with them. We need a heart that sees peoples' lives in the context of their eternal destiny, and we need to feel a sense of urgency for their salvation. We need a heart that loves people despite their weaknesses and faults, and despite the fact that they do not deserve it —a heart that wants to see God's Name glorified in their lives, and His kingdom extended; a heart of a missionary and 'kingdom builder'.

John Kelly and Paul Costa have made an impassioned plea for us to see ourselves as God's ministers and missionaries in the workplace, reminding us that, in the kingdom of God, none of us is a 'second class minister'. They remind us not to say, 'I'm only a student,' (or whatever our occupation may be.) Where you are is your mission field; that is where you can take charge for God and begin to build His kingdom.[1]

We need this sort of vision mixed with passion. We need the heart for it. Even if you have no desire now, do you want to ask God to *give* you the desire to answer the call?

Only the work of God in a believer's heart can stir up such love—a desire to see the lost come out of darkness and be firmly established in God's kingdom. Selwyn Hughes has written, 'The more God is allowed to evangelise the heart, the more effectively His influence can be spread through that heart to the world around.'[2] Only God working in the heart of Paul could have changed that hard man into someone who was prepared to suffer so that others would come to know Jesus through his witness. He saw himself as a witness for Jesus Christ, and he was prepared to endure trouble, work hard and demonstrate the character of Jesus in everything he did, so that his witness was effective. He made this clear:

> We put no stumbling block in anyone's path, so that our ministry will not be discredited. Rather, as servants of God we commend ourselves in every way: in great endurance; in troubles, hardships and distresses; in beatings, imprisonments and riots; in hard work, sleepless nights and hunger; in purity, understanding, patience and kindness; in the Holy Spirit and in sincere love; in truthful speech and in the power of God; with weapons of righteousness in the right hand and in the left....
>
> *2 Corinthians 6:3–7*

Paul's desire to be an effective witness was rooted in a heart that knew God, had experienced His grace, and wanted others to know Him. He saw himself primarily as a witness for God, and that was the calling he was committed to fulfilling through

---

[1] In *End Time Warriors*, Renew Books, 1999
[2] In *A New Heart*, Kingsway, 1982

his daily life. That was his passion; and all the short-term difficulties and frustrations were nothing in the light of the prospect of eternal salvation for others and the extension of God's kingdom. Are we brave enough to ask God to put in us a heart for our work colleagues? Do you see yourself as someone who has been put in your workplace to be a witness for Jesus? Do you need to ask God to help you to begin to care about the eternal destiny of those around you at work? If so, there is no better time than now.

PRAY FOR NON-CHRISTIAN COLLEAGUES

If having a heart for workplace mission is seeing the need for God to act in the lives of those around us, then prayer is about asking Him to act, and asking Him with confidence and boldness. It is about asking Him to meet the needs in their lives in a way that only He can do. Prayer is a vital element of any work of Christian outreach or mission. Salvation is a miraculous work of a merciful God, and part of our role is to pray that He will have mercy upon the people we work with, and that He will reach out to them, draw them to Himself, and show them His salvation. Jesus encouraged us to pray for God to establish His kingdom: 'Your kingdom come, your will be done on earth as it is in heaven' (Matthew 6:10); and Paul prayed for the salvation of his fellow countrymen. Such prayer was part of Paul's life, and an expression of what was on his heart for them: 'Brothers, my heart's desire and prayer to God for the Israelites is that they may be saved' (Romans 10:1). However, the devil will oppose Christian witness, trying to maintain a grip on the lives of non-Christians so as to keep them in sin and darkness. Witness in the workplace is, therefore, a confrontation between the kingdom of God and the dominion and plans of the devil. Prayer provides the spiritual weapon for witness, because as we ask God to intervene, move and show His power, He acts—binding the powers of darkness and releasing His blessing. So a vital part of our witness is to pray against the works of the enemy in the lives of our colleagues, and to pray for God to work in their lives—that He will bring them salvation. Prayer for our workmates is an essential key to seeing God's victory in their lives. There may be nobody else who has ever prayed for them—but God has brought them into contact with you.

God works powerfully in response to our prayers, and in the Scriptures we are repeatedly commanded to pray. All things are possible for Him, and He can turn anyone to Himself by the power of His Spirit. When Elijah prayed for rain after three and a half years of drought, the rain came and then there was life and a harvest. We may need to persevere in prayer for our colleagues before we see God move in their lives, but He encourages us to, 'ask and it will be given to you...' (Matthew 7:7) and to keep on asking: 'pray continually' (1 Thessalonians 5:17). Don Latham has found that prayer is essential if we are to see the kingdom of God extended in the workplace. He describes how praying for the sick at work has proved to be a powerful means of evangelism: 'We should pray for our friends and colleagues at work... I have discovered that once you start praying for individuals, things start to happen. One key area for me has been to pray for those who are sick. I can recount many stories of healing, often leading to the individuals coming to know Christ for themselves.'[1] We can start to pray for our workplace colleagues in simple ways, such as by writing down their names and praying through the list on a regular basis—both for their specific needs and for opportunities to get to know them and to share Jesus with them. We can pray for the Spirit to rain down on our workplace, and in faith believe that God will bring life and a harvest of souls, just as He brought rain when Elijah prayed.

SHOW THE REALITY OF JESUS BY THE WAY YOU WORK

> Whatever you do, work at it with all your heart, as working for the Lord, not for men, since you know that you will receive an inheritance from the Lord as a reward. It is the Lord Christ you are serving.
>
> *Colossians 3:23–24*

These verses remind us that whatever we happen to do as a job, as Christians we are to work with all our heart. The standard for

---

[1] Don Latham *Everyday Faith*, Terra Nova Publications, 2001

our work should be the very best we can achieve. Of course, this does not mean that we are to be perfectionists or workaholics. In an important sense, our 'employer' is the Lord our God. By working to a standard of excellence and giving our best, people will quickly see that we are different. We will also be pointing them to Him—because His work is always good, whether or not people are aware of it, or thankful for it. As you point people to Him you are doing the work of an evangelist.

DEMONSTRATE THE REALITY OF JESUS BY WHO YOU ARE

Ultimately, the quality and power of our Christian witness will depend on the extent to which our heart, mind and character have been changed to be like Jesus, and how far this is reflected in what we do and say at work.

Simply by doing the things we have been considering earlier in this book, we are demonstrating the reality of Jesus Christ. By the purity of our lifestyle, by speaking positively, never negatively about others, by constantly forgiving, submitting to appropriate authority, and in all the other areas of positive ethical behaviour and works of grace and generosity, we are witnessing to the truth that is in us, which comes from Jesus. Our witness for God will be in the detail of what we do, because it is in what we say, how we work and how we conduct ourselves that people will piece together the clues that tell them what we are really like. If they see Jesus in this, then our witness can be effective. We will be the light to others that Jesus wants us to be:

> 'You are the light of the world. A city on a hill cannot be hidden. Neither do people light a lamp and put it under a bowl. Instead they put it on its stand, and it gives light to everyone in the house. In the same way, let your light shine before men, that they may see your good deeds and praise your Father in heaven.'
>
> *Matthew 5:14–16*

People who shine with the qualities of Christ in the context of positive working relationships, consistently and over time, even when tested in adverse circumstances such as opposition from others, will be the light to others that Jesus was talking about. People who shine with godly qualities will be making him real to others, for:

> ...the fruit of the Spirit is love, joy, peace, patience, kindness, goodness, faithfulness, gentleness and self-control.
>
> *Galatians 5:22–23*

It may all seem a tall order, a tremendously high standard. But the Lord will produce in us more and more of the fruit of the Spirit if we allow Him to deal with us and continue changing us. As representatives of the qualities of Jesus in our workplace, we may have fallen short, but we can repent, ask God for forgiveness; and ask Him to make us the ambassadors for Christ that He wants us to be. There is a new start every day for each of us, and our weaknesses can become His opportunities. The transforming work of God in our life is a powerful witness, changing us to be more Christ-like. Working life presents an excellent opportunity for us to be witnesses, as people who know us well will notice any change in us. If we allow the Holy Spirit to go on changing us, we will shine brighter for Jesus, whatever our work calling.

LOVE JESUS AND SAY WHAT YOU WANT

What we say is at the heart of our Christian witness, because what we say reflects what is in our heart.

> ...out of the overflow of the heart the mouth speaks. The good man brings good things out of the good stored up in him, and the evil man brings evil things out of the evil stored up in him.
>
> *Matthew 12:34–35*

We have noted that what we say has an impact on others, either for good or bad. If we speak good things from our heart, there will be a good effect on those around us. By speaking positively about others, the company we work for, and our circumstances, and as we say things that encourage and make people feel valued, we will sow positive things into their lives, and have a beneficial impact on the way things are done in our workplace. All this is absolutely vital to effective witness. Being 'salt' to others is about making life more palatable, easier to bear and more enjoyable. It is about adding flavour, and enhancing peoples' experience of life. If our speech and conversation are to be 'salt' to others, it will help them see things more positively. By dwelling on what is good and encouraging, we will inspire hope in the often mundane circumstances of daily life. Our speech will be fresh. It is partly through what we say that we will fulfil the calling Jesus has given us all: 'You are the salt of the earth' (Matthew 5:13).

It is worth reflecting on what sort of things we say during the course of our working day, in the light of our desire to witness. The Christian who can tactfully speak something different from the crowd (without irritating everybody in the process) will be noticed and even liked. In this way, we will not only contribute to changing the company atmosphere and culture, but will also point people to Jesus Christ.

If we find it a struggle to keep our speech and conversation in the workplace acceptable to God, then we will need to go back to what is in our heart and ask Him to cleanse us. Peter, for example, encourages us all to purify our hearts and speech: 'Therefore, rid yourselves of all malice and all deceit, hypocrisy, envy and slander of every kind' (1 Peter 2:1). We need to repent of any malice, resentment, pride, deceit, or envy, or whatever it is in our hearts that is reflected outwardly in our speech. Once our heart is clean, then clean things can flow out of it, through our speech and conversation, and touch others. Our love for the Lord, and our relationship with Him, should shine through in our speech. If we love Him, then we will naturally want to be like Him, do as He does and walk in His ways. We should, therefore, love Him with all our heart then say what we like; because if we really love Him and know Him then our speech will be a credit to Him.

What we say, and how we respond to people in our speech and conversation, will make all the difference in the world. It will either point people to God and prove our Christian witness, or it will undermine and negate our witness completely, convincing them that they were right all along about Christians and Christianity.

SHOW THE DIFFERENCE THAT
KNOWING GOD CAN MAKE

Knowing God should make a real difference. It should make us stand out from those who do not know Him. We looked at the biblical accounts of the lives of Daniel and Joseph, and saw how knowing God made a real difference to them. They had wisdom, knowledge and understanding that others did not have, and so were able to solve the real problems and issues of the day. They had access to the powerful Almighty God who protected them in times of threat and adversity, and who prospered them. People saw their witness. When Daniel was pulled from the lion's den, the king honoured Daniel's God, and decreed that others throughout the land should fear and revere Him. They brought their faith in God into their workplace. However, for many of us our working life and our relationship with God are completely separate. We 'leave God at home' or in our church. What a difference it would make if we brought our faith in God into all aspects of our work and workplace!

If we seek God for the insights, the wisdom, and the revelation of knowledge that will help solve the key problems facing our team, our work area or the whole company, then He may give us some insight, some practical wisdom and some revelation that will be of real benefit, making our witness more powerful and effective for Him. He did so for Daniel, because he asked, and He did so for Joseph. So ask God to make you more useful to your employer—and exercise the spiritual gifts which God gives you. The witness of Daniel and Joseph was powerful when people could see that because they knew God they could offer more to their employer than other people, much more than just their natural abilities and efforts. Knowing God should make a real difference.

God is our help, and His help can bring us success in the day-to-day tasks that we face. However, if you are like me you will often forget that simple truth and try to get things done through your own abilities and sheer hard work. Often we leave too little room for God's power and grace to work. As the day goes on, the reality of His grace and help being freely available can fade from our minds, and by the end of the day we can be just as frustrated, 'wound up' and exhausted as our non-Christian colleagues. But God will help us if we ask. He can bring us success—which bears testimony to the God who helps His children and who can work so powerfully in our day to day lives. Consider again Abraham's servant. When Abraham was old, he asked his chief servant to go back to his native country and find a wife for his son, Isaac. What a responsibility, given that the promise of God's blessing for the nations was to be realised through Isaac and his offspring. But his servant took on the task and set off. Reaching Nahor, he rested in the evening with his camels, beside a well. This was the time the women of the town would come to draw water from the spring. Abraham's servant then did something profoundly simple, but extremely effective. He asked God to give him success in his job:

> "O Lord, God of my master Abraham, give me success today, and show kindness to my master Abraham."
>
> *Genesis 24:12*

He asked God to show him which girl was to be Isaac's wife. God answered his prayer, gave him success and it all worked out well. He received help from God in successfully completing his job, because he asked with the right motive—to bring success and honour to his boss, and to see God's purpose fulfilled. He asked because he knew that God would and could help. As for us, we too can pray for His help as we face the tasks and challenges of our working day. We should be success-minded. If we are walking right with the Lord, then we should expect success in our life and have a healthy and positive expectation that we will experience His favour. Of course, there may be times when we experience setbacks and difficulties, but we should believe that God really is working all things out for good. As we travel to work, we too can ask Him to give us success in the day ahead:

> *'O Lord, give me success today for the benefit of my boss, the company and my family, and for the greatness of your Name.'*

Since I read about Abraham's servant, I pray this every day, on my way to work. When we do that with the right motive in our hearts, God can demonstrate His power to bring success that could not be achieved through our natural abilities alone.

Experiencing the favour of God in the form of success in our work will get noticed. When Joseph was at Potiphar's house, his master could see that God was alive and real, and at work in Joseph's daily life:

> The Lord was with Joseph and he prospered, and he lived in the house of his Egyptian master. When his master saw that the Lord was with him and that the Lord gave him success in everything he did, Joseph found favour in his eyes and became his attendant.
>
> *Genesis 39:2–4*

Of course, Joseph experienced times of adversity, but God gave him success. When we know God ourselves, we point others to Him.

SHARING THE GOSPEL

Being an effective witness in the workplace is about shining for God, not about 'bashing people over the head' with Bible verses, nor about trying to persuade people to become Christians by our clever arguments or set-formula methods. However, there is a time and place for sharing the gospel and the word of God— should the opportunity open up for us, and should the person be ready and willing to listen. Whilst it is good to point people to Jesus by who we are, by how we work and by what we say, there is also a need to help them grasp the truth of the gospel directly, and to bring them to a full understanding of the Christian faith. Those with whom we work cannot simply guess what becoming a Christian involves; we have to be ready to explain it to them.

SUMMARY OF KEY POINTS

1. The workplace is a much neglected mission field for the good news of Jesus Christ. We, as Christians, need a vision and passion from God to see His kingdom established in the workplace.

2. Witness in the workplace is not about mechanically implementing a particular *method* or process. It is about manifesting Jesus in practical ways that have an impact on other people and the working world around us. It is about living *out* the reality of Christ *in* us.

3. We serve the infinite, powerful God who wants to extend His kingdom. We need to ask Him to show His reality and power right where we are, in our workplaces.

QUESTIONS FOR REFLECTION/DISCUSSION

1. Think about someone at work whom people seem to like or respect. What is it about their character or behaviour that tends to make people respect them?

2. Think about someone at work whom people seem to dislike, or for whom they lack respect. What is it about their character or behaviour that tends to make people feel that way about them?

3. Think of a time when someone said something encouraging to you or showed you some kindness at work. How did it make you feel about yourself, and about the other person?

4. Read 2 Corinthians 5:20–21. What sort of behaviour and attitude of the heart is needed for effective witness in your workplace?

5. What are some simple and practical things that you can do at work to show people the love and reality of Jesus in your life?

6. If you were to start praying for the salvation of some of your colleagues, who would you include on your prayer list? Where in your daily schedule could you most easily build in some prayer time for your colleagues on a regular basis?

7. In what ways could the gifts of the Holy Spirit help you to be an effective witness in your workplace?

8. List the ways in which anything from this chapter or from your review of the above questions applies to you as a working person in your own circumstances. Then list any **actions** you will take as a result of this study (e.g. further study or reflection, prayer, speaking to someone, requests for help, changing something about yourself) and be as specific as possible about **when** you will complete the action(s).

16

LET US RUN THE RACE

The writer of Hebrews encourages all Christians to '...run with perseverance the race marked out for us' (Hebrews 12:1). The challenge set before each of us is to fulfil God's plan for our lives—including our working lives. Throughout this book we have seen that His calling to be champions at work is a call to us all; not to a select few, but to ordinary people like you and me in offices, factories, shops, and hospitals—wherever He has positioned us. Never doubt that **you** really **can** be a champion for Him wherever you are and whatever work you do. He will help you if you are open to His help. He will challenge you, if you are open to His challenge. He will train you and change you—if you are open to Him leading you, and to Him working in your life. If you respond to His call, then He will bring victory in your working life and use you to extend His kingdom.

Every day, as you worship and adore Jesus, enjoy the precious relationship with your heavenly Father, and open yourself to being continually filled with the Holy Spirit, He will equip you with the vision and power to fulfil His call. He will provide you with everything you need to advance His kingdom in your place of work and to finish the race marked out for you. When I see Him, I want to hear Him say to me, 'Well done, good and faithful servant', and win the prize for completing the race. Is that something you want, too? You may want to pray along with me:

Father God, help me truly to be a champion for you in every part of my working life. Fill me with your Holy Spirit. Guide me in all I do each day. Give me wisdom, direction, true vision of your purposes, faithfulness to your word, and self-control in my thinking, speech and actions. Show me your opportunities by your prompting; open my ears to hear your voice; and, above all, I ask you to give me the compassion of Jesus for those who do not yet know him.

Amen

SUGGESTIONS FOR FURTHER READING

J. Carr, *Vision* (Charis, 1989)

S. Chalke & P. Relph, *Managing your Time* (Kingsway, 1998)

P. Y. Cho, *Prayer: Key to Revival* (Word, 1984)

P. Curran, *All the Hours God Sends?* (IVP, 2000)

S. Green, *Serving God? Serving Mammon? Christians in the Financial Markets* (Marshall Pickering, 1996)

Mark Greene, *Thank God it's Monday: Ministry in the Workplace* (SU, 1997)

S. Hughes, *A New Heart* (Kingsway, 1982)

B. Hybels, *Faith in the Real World* (Hodder and Stoughton, 1996)

L.B. Jones, *Jesus, CEO: Using Ancient Wisdom for Visionary Leadership* (Hyperion, 1995)

L. Kaufman & M. Quigley, *And What Do You Do? When Women Choose to Stay Home* (Wildcat Canyon, 2000)

J. Kelly & P. Costa, *End Time Warriors* (Renew, 1999)

L. Lambert, *Preparation for the Coming of the Lord* (Christian Tape Ministry, 4424 Huguenot Road, Richmond, Virginia 23235, 1990)

D. Latham, *A Faith that Works* (Terra Nova Publications, 1997)

D. Latham, *Being Unmistakably Christian at Work* (Terra Nova Publications, 2000)

D. Latham, *Everyday Faith: Applying the Sermon on the Mount to the Workplace* (Terra Nova Publications, 2001)

Brother Lawrence, *The Practice of the Presence of God* Trans. E. M. Blaiklock (Hodder and Stoughton, 1981)

R. Mattox, *The Christian Employee* (Bridge Publishing, 1978)

A. L. McGinnis, *The Friendship Factor* (Augsburg, 1979)

B. Mumford, *Entering and Enjoying Worship* (Manna, 1975)

B. Patterson, *Serving God by What We Do* (IVP, 1994)

B. Patterson, *Work and Worship: Serving God in Everything You Do* (IVP, 1994)

L. Peabody, *Secular Work is Full Time Service* (CLC, 1974)

T. Peters & R. H. Waterman Jr., *In Search of Excellence* (HarperCollins Business, 1982)

A. Richardson, *The Biblical Doctrine of Work* (SCM, 1952)

H. Sala, *Heroes: People Who Made a Difference in Our World* (OMF, 1998)

C. Schumacher, *God in Work* (Lion, 1998)

D. Sherman, *Spiritual Warfare for every Christian* (Frontline Communications, 1990)

D. Sherman & W. Hendricks, *Your Work Matters to God* (The Navigators, Singapore, 1987)

S. A. Steele, *Choosing to Change* (Gospel Light, 1998)

B. Subritzky, *Receiving the Gifts of The Holy Spirit* (Sovereign World, 1985)

C. Swindoll, *A Man of Integrity and Forgiveness: Joseph* (Word, 1998)

S. Terkel, *Working* (Pantheon, 1972)

K. Tondeur, *Your Money and Your Life* (Triangle, 1996)

K. Tondeur, *What Jesus said about Money and Possessions* (Monarch, 1998)

Transformed Working Life: Study Notes (International Christian Chamber of Commerce ACT Ltd, c/o 277 Fleet Road, Fleet, Hants GU13 8BT)

M. Volf, *Work in the Spirit: Towards a Theology of Work* (OUP, 1991)

S. Walton, *A Call to Live: Vocation for Everyone* (Triangle, 1994)

M. West, *Creativity and Innovation at Work* in *The Psychologist*, Sept. 2000, vol. XIII, No. 9, 460–464 (published by The British Psychological Society)

BEING UNMISTAKABLY CHRISTIAN AT WORK

Don Latham

The author writes:

'Arriving at work in the early morning, I would pray. Walking round the office, before the staff came to work, I would speak the presence of God, the Spirit of God, into the building. I prayed that people would want to come and work there; that they would want to succeed with me; that it would be a good place to work; that there would be harmony, unity, creativity. We need to do this. I prayed for my colleagues. I prayed that in me, and in other Christian brothers and sisters on the staff — individually and corporately — they would see a reflection of Jesus; that they would see something that might attract them to him.'

Don Latham has a wealth of experience as a local authority Chief Executive, an independent consultant, and non-executive Director in the Health Service. A well-known Christian speaker, he has taught at SPRING HARVEST.

ISBN 1-90194906-0

£3.50

EVERYDAY FAITH

Don Latham

How we can put into practice in our workplaces
the teaching of Jesus in the Sermon on the Mount

The author writes:

'The solid foundation for our life is the word of
God. When the temptations, tests and trials come, then
the strength of our foundations will be revealed.'

For many people the trials and temptations are found amidst
the demands and stresses of their work.

You may wonder whether it is possible not just to cope, but to
be SALT and LIGHT at work

— without worry or anxiety
— without judging others
— with God's wisdom concerning the problem areas
— praying effectively, for needs of colleagues and the
  work itself
— witnessing appropriately
— exercising practical faith and discernment, with
  honesty and integrity.

If all this sounds 'out of reach', EVERYDAY FAITH shows
that these things are possible, if we learn and apply the
teaching of Jesus.

ISBN 1-90194910-9

£3.50